P9-BYR-783

THE MUSIC BOOK

Eunice Boardman
Professor of Music Education
University of Wisconsin
Madison, Wisconsin

Barbara Andress
Professor of Music Education
Arizona State University
Tempe, Arizona

Music Consultant
Buryl Red
Composer, Arranger, and Conductor

Special Consultants

William Anderson
Professor of Music Education
and Ethnomusicology
Assistant Dean
of the Graduate College
Kent State University
Kent, Ohio

Mervin W. Britton
Professor of Music
Arizona State University
Tempe, Arizona

Virginia Garrison
Teacher, Consultant
Richmond County Schools
Cape Breton Island
Nova Scotia

William Hughes
Professor of Music Education
Florida State University
Tallahassee, Florida

Beth Landis
Former Director of Music Education
City Schools
Riverside, California

Betty Welsbacher
Director, Special Music Education
Wichita State University
Wichita, Kansas

Holt, Rinehart and Winston, Publishers
New York, Toronto, London, Sydney

Consultants

Martha Mahoney
Elementary Music Department Head
Elementary Schools
Milford, Connecticut

Donald Regier
Supervisor of Vocal Music
Secondary Schools
Baltimore County, Maryland

Keith Thompson
Associate Professor, Music Education
Pennsylvania State University
University Park, Pennsylvania

Nelmatilda Woodard
Director, Bureau of Music Education
Board of Education
City of Chicago

Portions of this book previously published in EXPLORING MUSIC 7
Copyright © 1975, 1971 by Holt, Rinehart and Winston, Publishers

Copyright © 1981 by Holt, Rinehart and Winston, Publishers
All rights reserved
Printed in the United States of America

ISBN: 0-03-042231-0
01234   039   987654321

ACKNOWLEDGMENTS

Grateful acknowledgment is given to the following authors and publishers:

• Ahab Music Company, Inc., for "Everything Is Beautiful." Copyright © 1970 by Ahab Music Company, Inc. Used by permission.

• Alfred Publishing Co., for "Kathy's Cookin'" from *Instant Improvisation* by Tom Ferguson. Used by permission.

• American Ethical Union for "Brethern In Peace Together," from *We Sing Of Peace*. Copyright © 1955. The American Union Catalog Number 54:11625. Used by permission.

• April-Blackwood Music for "Spinning Wheel," by David Clayton Thomas. Copyright © 1968 by Blackwood Music Inc., and Bay Music Ltd. All rights reserved. Used by permission.

• Arc Music Corporation for "Reelin' and Rockin'." Words and music by Chuck Berry. Copyright © 1958 by Arc Music Corporation, 110 East 59th Street, New York, N.Y. 10019. Used by permission.

• Bibo Music Publishers for "Gonna Get Along Without You Now," by Milton Kellum. Copyright © 1952 by Bibo Music Publishers. Copyright renewed. International copyright secured. All rights reserved. Used by permission.

• Big Three Music Co., Inc., for "Five Hundred Miles," by Hedy West. Copyright © 1961, 1962 by Atzal Music, Inc. All rights controlled by UniChappell Music, Inc. (Rightsong Publishers). All rights reserved. Used by permission.

• Fred Bock Music Company for "Scarborough Fair." Copyright © 1969 by Gentry Publications; for "The Tree of Peace," Copyright © 1970 by Fred Bock Music Company. All rights reserved. Used by permission.

• Chappell Music Company for "Goin' Down To Town," "The Cruel War," "Sucking Cider Through A Straw," "Turkey In The Straw," "Hard, Ain't It Hard," and "Mama Don't 'Low." Copyright © 1975 by Chappell & Co. Inc. International Copyright Secured. All Rights Reserved. Used by Permission.

• Chappell Music Company for "I Walk The Line." Copyright © 1956 by Hi Lo Music, Inc. All rights administered by Unichappel Music, Inc. (Rightsong Music, Publishers). International Copyright Secured. All Rights Reserved. Used by permission.

• Cherry Lane Music Co., for "Deep Fork River Blues," by Tom Paxton. Copyright © 1962 by Cherry Lane Music Co. This arrangement copyrighted © 1981 Cherry Lane Music Co. All rights reserved. Used by permission.

• Cherry Lane Music Co., for "I Write The Songs," words and music by Bruce Johnston. Copyright © 1974 by Artists Music, Inc. This arrangement copyrighted © 1981 by Artists Music, Inc. All rights throughout the world administered by *Interworld Music Group, Inc.*, 8304 Beverly Boulevard, Los Angeles, California 90048. All rights reserved. Used by permission.

• Duane Music Company for "Wish I Knew How It Would Feel To Be Free," by Billy Taylor. Copyright © 1964 by Duane Music Company. Used by permission.

• Ensign Music Corporation for (Good Old Electric) Washing Machine. Words and music by John Hartford. Copyright © 1967 by Ensign Music Corporation. Used by permission.

• European American Music Distributors Corp. for "De Natura Sonoris" by Krzysztof Penderecki. Copyright © 1967 by Moeck Verlag, Celle/FRG. Used by permission of European American Music Distributors Corp. sole U.S. agent for Moeck Verlag, Celle/FRG.

• Fall River Music Inc. for "Guantanamera." Original lyrics and music by José Fernandez Dias (Joseito Fernandez). Music adaptation by Pete Seeger. Lyric adaptation by Hector Angulo, based on a poem by José Marti. Copyright © 1963, 1965 by Fall River Music Inc. All rights reserved. Used by permission.

• Carl Fischer, Inc., for "Gaudeamus Hodie" ((Let Us Rejoice Today), words and music by Natalie Sleeth. Copyright © 1972 by Carl Fischer, Inc., New York. International Copyright Secured. All rights reserved. Used by permission.

• Folkways Music Publishers, Inc., for "Tear Down The Walls." Words and music by Fred Neil. TRO-Copyright © 1964 and 1965 Folkways Music Publishers, Inc., New York, N.Y. Used by permission.

• Fox Fanfare Music, Inc., for "Ease On Down The Road," by Charlie Smalls. Copyright © 1974, 1975 & 1977 by Fox Fanfare Music, Inc. All rights reserved. Used by permission.

• Generic Music for "Suliram," and "Go Down, Moses." Copyright © 1971 by Generic Music. "Hava Nagila." Copyright © 1972 by Generic Music. "Skip to My Lou." Copyright © 1981 by Generic Music. "Bell Gloria." Copyright © 1970 by Generic Music. "Wayfarin' Stranger." Copyright © 1971 by Generic Music. "The Tiger." Copyright © 1980 Generic Music. All rights reserved. Used by permission.

• Hansen Publications, Inc., for "It Ain't Gonna Rain No More." Copyright © 1970 by California Music Press. Used by permission.

• International Music Company for "Clair de Lune" from Suite Bergamasque. Copyright © 1961. Used by permission.

• Jobete Music Company, Inc., for "A Place In The Sun," by Byron Wells and Ronald Miller. Copyright © 1966 by Jobete Music Company, Inc. Used by permission.

• Liveright Publishing Corporation for "stinging gold worms" from TULIPS & CHIMNEYS by E. E. Cummings, edited by George James Firmage. Copyright 1923, 1925, renewed 1951, 1953 by E. E. Cummings. Copyright © 1973, 1976 by Nancy T. Andrews. Copyright © 1973, 1976 by George James Firmage. Used by permission.

• Northern Songs Limited for "When I'm Sixty-four." Copyright © 1967 by Northern Songs Limited. All rights reserved. Used by permission.

• Peer International Corporation for "Hurdy Gurdy Man," and "Get Thy Bearings." Copyright © 1968 by Donovan (Music) Ltd. Sole selling Agent Peer International Corporation. Used by permission.

• Prestige Records, Inc., for the "Ramblin' Jack Elliott" recording of the lyrics for "The Cuckoo." E. Lowell Rogers for arrangement of "Delta Dawn." Used by permission.

• Stormking Music Inc., for "The Dove," by Ewan MacColl. Copyright © 1960 by Stormking Music Inc. All rights reserved. Used by permission.

• G. Schirmer, Inc., for "I Wonder As I Wander." Copyright 1934 by G. Schirmer, Inc. Used by permission.

• Tree Publishing Co., Inc., for "Green Green Grass of Home," by Curly Putman. Copyright © 1965 by Tree Publishing Co. Inc. This arrangement copyrighted © 1981 by Tree Publishing Co., Inc. Used by permission.

• Trigon Music, a division of Triune Music Inc., for "If We Don't Make It Work, Who Will?" Copyright © 1974 by Trigon Music. International copyright secured. All rights reserved. Used by permission.

• United Artists Music Co. Inc., for "Good Morning Starshine." Copyright © 1966, 1967, 1968 by James Redo, Gerome Ragni, Galt MacDermot, Nat Shapiro and United Artists Music Co. Inc. For "Oh Happy Day," by Edwin R. Hawkins. Copyright © 1969 by Kama Rippa Music, Inc. and Edwin R. Hawkins Music Co. For "Delta Dawn," by Alex Harvey and Larry Collins. Copyright © 1972 United Artists Music Co., Inc. and Big Ax Music. All rights administered by United Artists Music Co., Inc. Used by permission.

• Warner Bros. for "Turn Around, Look At Me." Copyright © 1961 Warner-Tamerlane Publishing Corp., Hill and Range Songs, Inc., Elvis Presley Music, Inc. Gladys Music, Inc. All rights administered by Warner-Tamerlane Publishing Corp. All rights reserved. Used by permission.

• World Around Songs for "Bwana, IBariki Afrika." English translation copyrighted © 1958 by Cooperative Recreation Service, Inc. Used by permission of World Around Songs, Burnsville, N. C. 28714.

PHOTO CREDITS

All HRW Photos by Russell Dian except for the following: p. 0–1–HRW Photo by Ken Lax; p. 3–1–right HRW photo by Ken Lax; p. 18–1–The Hispanic Society of America; p. 39–1–Tom Hollyman/Photo Researchers; p. 40–1–Max Tharpe/Monkmeyer; p. 75–1–George Holton/Photo Researchers; p. 77–1–Andy Levin/Black Star; p. 77–2–John Reggero; p. 77–3–Andy Levin/Black Star p. 77–4–Bob Fitch/Black Star; p. 90–1–12–HRW Photos by Ken Lax; p. 114–2–NYPL.

Additional copyright information and photo credits appear with the materials used.

ART CREDITS

Tom Cardamone Advertising, Inc.
Illustrations by John Wallner

Editorial Development   Lois Eskin, Alice Trimmer, Cathy Y. Comins, Joan Sayevich
Editorial Processing   Margaret M. Byrne, Regina Chilcoat, Anne Drouillard
Art and Production   Vivian Fenster, Fred C. Pusterla, Robin M. Swenson, Russell Dian, Ira A. Goldner, Beth McNally, Barbara Orzech, Anita Dickhuth, Ellen Lokiec, Joan Marinelli, Amy Newberg
Audio/Visual Production   Robert Spivak, Martin Brooks
Product Manager   Charles Herbek
Researchers   Pamela Floch, Gerard LaVan
Consultants   Sheila Nettles, Ruth Spies
Advisory Board   John Eskew, John Boynton, Gary Crump, Jack Custer, Jim Dellisanti, Linda Lynch, Dennis Spurgeon

CONTENTS

Unit 1
MUSICAL TRADITIONS
The Oral Tradition

...a journey of ideas, words, and music...

CHART 1: Commitment to Musical Learning (1)	
In this section you will have an opportunity to participate in the oral tradition . . .	
learn melodies by hearing songs	learn to perform harmony by listening
create and share your own song	describe what you hear

- Which of these can you now do independently?
- In which of these areas will you commit yourself to becoming more independent?

- You hear the songs of today played repeatedly on your radio, TV, or stereo. The ones that are particularly meaningful to you are quickly learned.

  - When you learn music in this way you are sharing in an old tradition. People have always learned and passed on their most important ideas and feelings in this way from one generation to the next.

    - Through conversation, poetry, music, myths, and tales, people have orally communicated what was important to them.

- Passing information in this way is called learning through the **oral tradition.**

- Continue the **oral tradition:** listen to feelings and ideas expressed through song; repeat them and pass them on.

...from past,
to present, to future...

I WRITE THE SONGS

Words and Music by Bruce Johnston

I've been alive forever
And I wrote the very first song.
I am music and
I write the song.
I write the songs that make the whole world sing.
I write the songs of love and special things.
I write the songs that make the young girls cry.
I write the songs, I write the songs. . . .

Copyright © 1974 by Artists Music, Inc. All rights throughout the world administered by INTERWORLD MUSIC GROUP, INC., 8034 Beverly Boulevard, Los Angeles, CA 90048. Used by permission. All rights reserved.

Your Singing Voice

When you participate in the **oral tradition** through singing, you are engaging in an experience that will continue throughout your life. To enjoy singing, it will be helpful if you know more about your voice and how it changes from time to time.

Begin by finding your singing range.
- Sing "Skip to My Lou."

Skip, skip, skip to my Lou, Skip, skip, skip to my Lou...

Girls: Most girls will find this a comfortable singing range. You can sing melody or harmony parts. These parts will be called **Treble I** and **Treble II.** Each of you will want to learn **Treble I** on some songs and **Treble II** on others.

Fellows: Male voices will fall in different ranges. Some of your voices may be changing.

- Now, only fellows sing "Skip to My Lou."

Skip, skip, skip to my Lou, Skip, skip, skip to my Lou...

Your teacher may indicate to some of you to stop singing. If so, you are **Baritones.**

- Remaining fellows should sing "Skip to My Lou" again in this range:

Skip, skip, skip to my Lou, Skip, skip, skip to my Lou...

Your teacher may indicate to some of you to stop singing. If so, you are **Changing Voices.**

Those of you who are still singing are **Treble I** or **Treble II.** Your voices have not yet changed.

Form a group with others who are in your singing range.

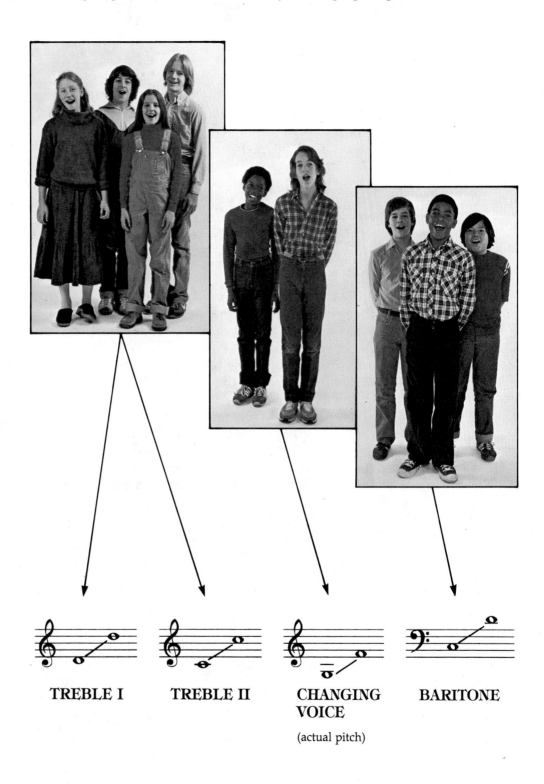

TREBLE I   TREBLE II   CHANGING
VOICE

BARITONE

(actual pitch)

Learn to sing parts especially arranged for your voice
range. Listen to the recording of "Skip to My Lou."
Then learn the special part that fits your voice range.

Share in the Oral Tradition

TEAR DOWN THE WALLS

Words and Music by Fred Neil

Listen to the recording. Choose the part that fits your range. Learn it by participating in the oral tradition.

Tear down the walls, Listen to freedom singin' out,
Tear down the walls, Can't you hear the church bells
   ringin' out?
Give ev'ry man the chance to take his brother's hand,
Tear down the walls, tear down the walls.

The music's ev'rywhere, wherever man is free,
The music's in the air that lights the road to liberty.

Tear down the walls, Listen to freedom ringin' out,
Tear down the walls, Can't you hear the church bells
   singin' out?
Let ev'ry man sing it over the land,
Tear down the walls, tear down the walls.

TRO—© Copyright 1964 & 1965 Folkways Music Publishers, Inc., New York, N.Y. Used by permission.

EASE ON DOWN THE ROAD

from "The Wiz"

Words and Music by Charlie Smalls

This song is performed in unison.
You will hear it performed in two different ranges.
Which range is appropriate for your voice?
Learn this song by participating in the oral tradition.

Come on, ease on down, ease on down the road.
Come on, ease on down, ease on down the road.
Don't you carry nothin' that might be a load.
Come on, ease on down, ease on down the road.

Come on, ease on down, ease on down the road.
Come on, ease on down, ease on down the road.
Don't you carry nothin' that might be a load.
Come on, ease on down, ease on down the road.

'Cause there may be times
    when you think you've lost your mind
And the steps you've taken
    leave you three, four steps behind.

Just you keep on keepin'
    on the road that you choose
And don't give up walkin'
    'cause you gave up shoes.

Pick your left foot up
    when your right one's down.
Come on legs keep movin',
    don't you lose no ground,

'Cause the road you're walkin'
    might be long sometime,
But just keep on steppin'
    and you'll be just fine.

Come on, ease on down, ease on down the road.
Come on, ease on down, ease on down the road.
Don't you carry nothin' that might be a load.
Come on, ease on down, ease on down the road.
(repeat and fade)

© 1974, 1975 & 1977 by Fox Fanfare Music Inc. All rights reserved. Used by permission.

The Message: MUSIC

When a composer creates music for a song, the musical ideas are chosen to convey feelings and to draw the listener into the music.

The composer may achieve this in various ways, including:

- stretching a word out over several pitches
- repeating a melodic idea
- repeating rhythm patterns
- creating a melody over a harmonic sequence

Which of these ways did Donovan Leitch use when he wrote "Hurdy Gurdy Man"?

HURDY GURDY MAN

Words and Music by Donovan Leitch

Thrown like a star in my vast sleep I open my eyes to take a
    peep
To find that I was by the sea, gazing with tranquility.

'Twas then when the Hurdy Gurdy Man came singing songs
    of love,
Then when the Hurdy Gurdy Man came singing songs of
    love.
Hurdy gurdy hurdy gurdy hurdy gurdy, gurdy he sang . . .
      (Repeat last line two more times.)

Histories of ages past unenlightened shadows cast
Down through all eternity, the crying of humanity.

'Tis then when the Hurdy Gurdy Man came singing songs
    of love,
Then when the Hurdy Gurdy Man came singing songs of
    love.
Hurdy gurdy hurdy gurdy hurdy gurdy, gurdy he sang . . .
      (Repeat last line two more times.)

Hurdy gurdy hurdy gurdy hurdy gurdy, gurdy he sang,
Here comes the roly poly man and he's singing songs of
    love,
Roly poly roly poly, poly roly poly he sang.
      (Repeat all three lines and fade.)

Copyright © 1968 by Donovan (Music) Ltd. Sole selling agent Peer International Corporation. Used by permission.

Listen to these songs. Which ways did the lyricist and composer use to communicate their message?

I WALK THE LINE

Words and Music by Johnny Cash

I keep a close watch on this heart of mine.
I keep my eyes wide open all the time.
I keep the ends out for the tie that binds.
Because you're mine, I walk the line.

I find it very very easy to be true.
I find myself alone when each day is through.
Yes, I'll admit that I'm a fool for you.
Because you're mine, I walk the line.

REELIN' AND ROCKIN'

Words and Music by Chuck Berry

Sometimes I will, then again I think I won't,
Sometimes I will, then again I think I won't,
Sometimes I do, then again I think I don't.

Looked at the clock and it was almost one,
I said, "Come on, baby, let's have us some fun."
We were reelin',
Reelin' and a rockin' and a rollin', baby.
We were reelin' and a rockin' and rollin' till the break of
     dawn.

The Message: WORDS

When a poet or lyricist writes words for a song, the words are carefully chosen to convey feelings and to draw the listener into those feelings. The lyricist may achieve this by deliberate use of:

- personal pronouns (such as "you" and "I")
- repetition of words and word patterns
- similes, metaphors, word pictures
- current slang expressions
- traditional expressions passed on from song to song

Which of these ways did Ronald Miller use when he wrote the lyrics for "A Place in the Sun"?

A PLACE IN THE SUN

Lyrics by Ronald Miller   Music by Bryan Wells

Sing the melody

Like a long, lonely stream I keep running towards a dream,

moving on, moving on.

Like a branch on a tree I keep reaching to be free,

moving on, moving on.

'Cause there's a place in the sun

where there's hope for everyone

where my poor restless heart's gotta run.

Listen and choose the part best suited to your voice.

There's a place in the sun

and before my life is done

got to find me a place in the sun.

Copyright © 1966 Jobete Music Company, Inc. Used by permission.

Your Own Message

Songs may be created in a variety of ways:

- beginning with the words
- beginning with a musical idea
- with words and music created at the same time.

When the same person creates both the words and the music, the song-maker might begin . . .

    . . . by strumming a guitar (or playing the piano) to find an appealing sequence of chords:
        G F C C G
    . . . by discovering an interesting rhythm pattern:

    . . . by creating lyrics:
        "Life is like a French fry without ketchup."
    . . . by finding a "hook" that combines key words and musical ideas:

When you're gone, gone, oh so gone.

A phrase from a song that was composed in these stages might result in the following:

Life is like a french fry with-out ketch-up

When you're gone, gone, oh so gone.

Choose one of these ways to create your own song—or combine several different ways!

The Message Transmitted

Many songs of today have their roots in the poetry and melodies of ancient times. As these songs have entered the **oral tradition,** changes have often occurred.

Segments of songs may be combined as the singer borrows a refrain from one . . . a phrase from another . . . a "story line" from a third.

Listen to "The Dove" and "The Cuckoo," two folk songs arranged in contemporary settings.

THE DOVE

Words by Ewan MacColl   Traditional

The dove she is a pretty bird, she sings as she flies,
She brings us glad tidings and tells us no lies.
She drinks the spring waters to make her voice clear
When her nest she is building and the summer is near.

Come all you young fellows, take warning by me,
Don't go for a soldier, don't join no army.
For the dove she will leave you, the raven will come,
And death will come marching at the beat of the drum.

Come all you pretty fair maids, come walk in the sun,
And don't let your young man ever carry a gun,
For the gun it will scare her, and she'll fly away,
And then there'll be weeping by night and by day.

The dove she is a pretty bird, she sings as she flies,
She brings us glad tidings, and tells us no lies.
She drinks the spring waters to make her voice clear
When her nest she is building and the summer is near.

© Copyright 1960 by Stormking Music Inc. All rights reserved. Used by permission.

THE CUCKOO

Words adapted by   Traditional
Jack Elliott

Well, the cuckoo is a pretty bird
And she warbles as she flies,
But the cuckoo never warbles
Till the fifth day of July.

I've gambled in England,
And I've gambled in Spain.
If I have to gamble,
I'll win your next game.

I'll build me a cabin
On a mountain so high,
So I can see Willie
As she passes by.

Well, the cuckoo is a pretty bird
And she warbles as she flies,
But the cuckoo never warbles
Till the fifth day of July.

Did the singers of the songs on pages 10 and 11 participate in the oral tradition?

Before you answer this question, listen to an Appalachian song and two early English folk songs.

- What have the contemporary folk singers borrowed?
- What have they changed?

THE CUCKOO

Traditional Appalachian Folk Song

The cuckoo is a funny bird, she sings as she flies.
She'll bring you glad tidings, she'll tell you no lies.
She sips from the pretty flowers to make her voice clear,
And she'll never sing cuckoo
    till the spring of the year.

THE CUCKOO

Traditional English Folk Song

O the cuckoo she's a pretty bird, she singeth as she flies;
She bringeth good tidings, she telleth no lies.
She sucketh white flowers, for to keep her voice clear;
And the more she singeth cuckoo,
    the summer draweth near.

THE TURTLE DOVE

Traditional English Folk Song

O don't you see that little tiny dove,
Sitting under yonder tree?
Lamenting of her own true love,
    And so shall I for thee, my dear,
    And so shall I for thee.

DELTA DAWN

Arranged by Lowell Rogers

Words and Music by Alex Harvey
and Larry Collins

How accurate were you in learning the songs in this chapter by **listening** only? Did you find that many repeated listenings were necessary?

This time, learn "Delta Dawn" by using the visual description of the rhythm and melody as a clue.

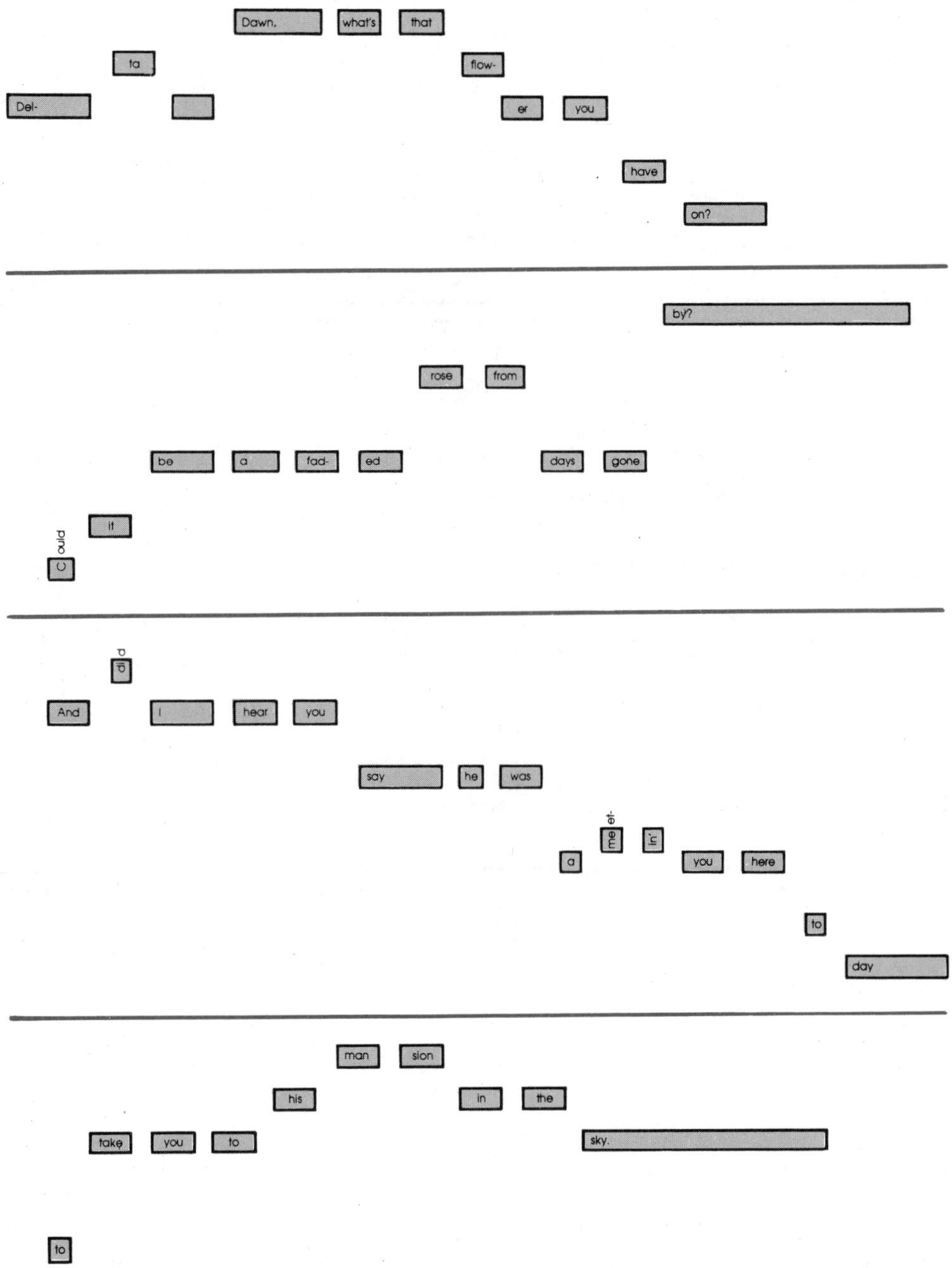

Dawn, what's that

ta

flow-

Del- er you

have

on?

by?

rose from

be a fad- ed days gone

ould
C it

to
a

And i hear you

say he was

me et-
in
a you here

to

day

man sion

his in the

take you to sky.

to

Listen again to "Delta Dawn." This time, listen carefully as the refrain is performed in harmony. Choose the part that best fits your vocal range. Follow the visual description to help you learn your part.

1

F   Bb   F

Delta Dawn, what's that flower you have on?

C

Could it be a faded rose from days gone

by?

F   Bb   F

did I hear you say he was a meetin' you here today

And

C   F

to take you to his mansion   sky.

in the

3

F   Bb   F

flower you have

Delta Dawn, what's that   on?

C

Could it be a faded rose from days gone

by?

F   Bb   F

meetin' you here to

did I hear you say he was a   day

And

C   F

to take you to his mansion   sky.

in the

5

F   Bb   F

flower you have

Delta Dawn, what's that   on?

C

Could it be a faded rose from days gone by?

F   Bb   F

meetin' you here to

And did I hear you say he was a   day

C   F

to take you to his mansion in the sky.

Hearing Others Sing

Singing is one of the most important ways in which people make music.

Meanings may be expressed through the use of words or unique vocal sounds.

"Sound Patterns" is performed by a chorus using unusual vocal sounds.

What unusual sounds do you hear? Describe them on your chart.

SOUND PATTERNS

by Pauline Oliveros

Mouth Sounds

Musical Controls

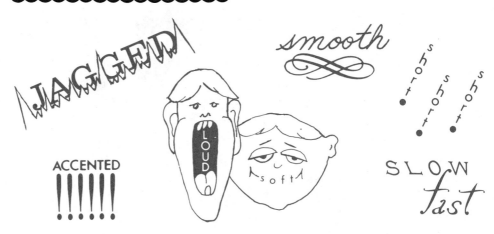

Create a Choral Piece

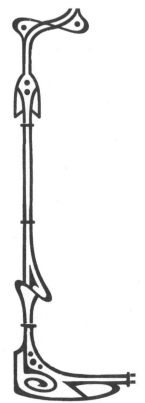

stinging
gold swarms
upon the spires
silver

       chants the litanies the
great bells are ringing with rose
the lewd fat bells

         and a tall

wind
is dragging
the
sea

with

dream

-S

         by e. e. cummings

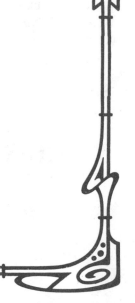

- Use this poem to create a composition for chorus.
- Work in small groups to plan the composition. Then use the class as your chorus and perform your work.
- Plan your piece. Will you create a simple melody for the words? Will you add harmony? Will you use unusual vocal sounds?
- How can you most dramatically have the chorus express words such as:

STINGING   SWARMS   **GREAT BELLS**

TALL   WIND   **dragging**   **DREAMS**

- Write your music plan on a separate sheet of paper.

CIRCLES

        by Luciano Berio

Listen to Luciano Berio's setting of this same poem.
Were the ideas of your group and those of Berio similar or
very different?

Pass a Song Along

Set up a "recording studio" near the classroom. Your studio should be located so that others in the classroom cannot hear what is going on.

- **STUDENT 1** Go to the recording studio.
  Make up a song and record it.

- **STUDENT 2** Join **Student 1.**
  Listen while **Student 1** sings his or her song twice.
  Then sing it to yourself.

- **STUDENT 1** Return to the classroom.

- **STUDENT 3** Join **Student 2.**
  Listen while **Student 2** sings **Student 1's** song twice.
  Then sing it yourself.

- **STUDENT 2** Return to the classroom.

Continue this procedure until the song has been passed through several singers.

- **LAST SINGER** Record the song.
  Bring the tape recorder to the classroom.

- **EVERYONE** Listen to the original and final versions of the song.
  How accurately did you pass the song along?
  Why are many versions of songs passed on through the oral tradition?

The Written Tradition

CHART 3: Commitment to Musical Learning (2)	
Within this section you will have an opportunity to participate in the written tradition . . .	
read rhythms from notation	sing a harmonizing part from notation
read melodies from notation	associate what you see with what you hear

- Which of these can you now do independently?
- In which of these areas will you commit yourself to becoming more independent?

Follow a Scope

Perform this choral composition by reading the score.

- Each person chooses a starting pitch.
- Each person sings sustained sounds on "oo," "ah," "ay," or "ee."
- Memorize the score. Close your eyes. Begin to sing.

A time line has now been added to the score. Perform it again.
This time, follow the score as a conductor counts seconds aloud.

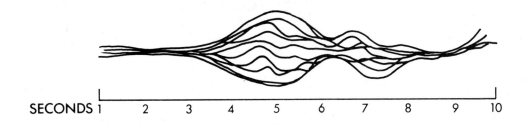

Perform the work a third time, using the added information.

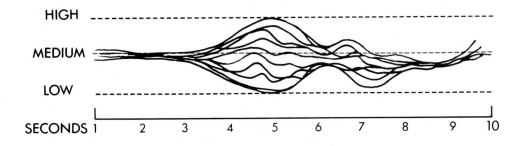

The score now provides some information about **duration** and **pitch.**
How might you add information about dynamic contrasts?
Prepare your own score of this piece. Perform the composition once more.

THE TIGER

Words excerpted from
"The Tiger" by William Blake

Music by Buryl Red

A "cluster" or the sign 𝄐 indicates a group of tones sung at the same time. The pitches should be close together. The singers choose their own pitches.

The sign 𝄐 indicates a spoken sound.

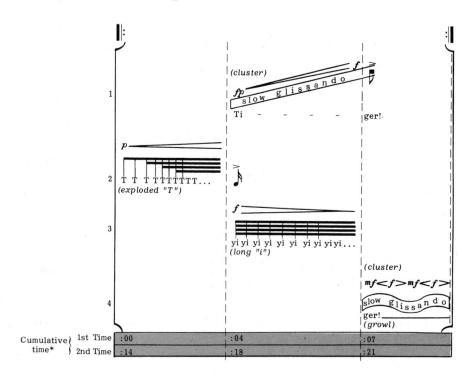

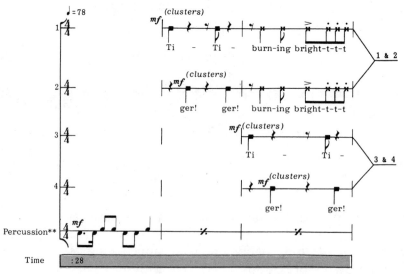

* Time is approximate, decided by director.
** Drum sounds such as log drum, talking drum, bongos, congas, or tom toms.

Copyright © 1980 Generic Music. All rights reserved. Used by permission.

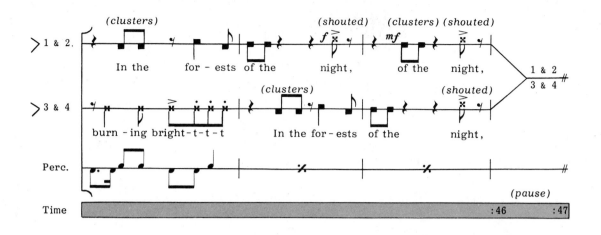

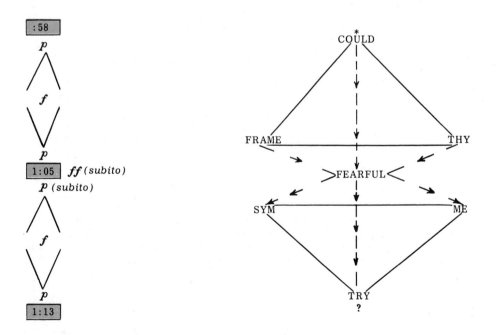

* Voices begin this section at the same time.
     • Each person chooses to start with word shown at any point of upper triangle.
     • Speak words in any order and at any speed.
     • Follow time span and dynamics as shown at left.
  All voices converge on "FEARFUL" at conductor's cue.
  Follow same procedure for lower triangle as with the upper one to end the composition, speaking syllables in any order.

DE NATURA SONORIS

(excerpt)

by Krzysztof Penderecki

Can you follow this contemporary score as you listen? What notational devices does the composer use to communicate his ideas?

What do you think these symbols might mean?

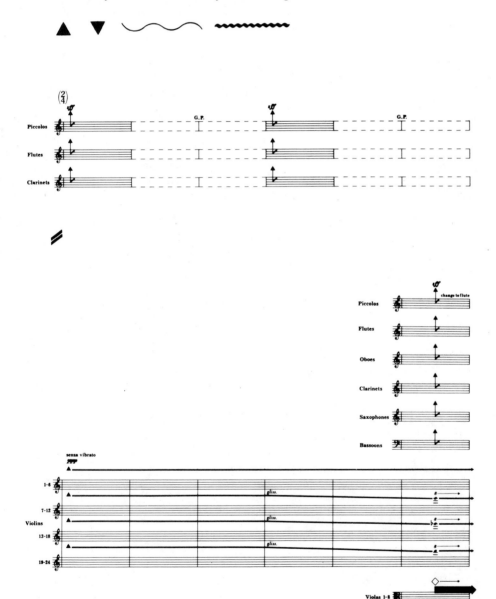

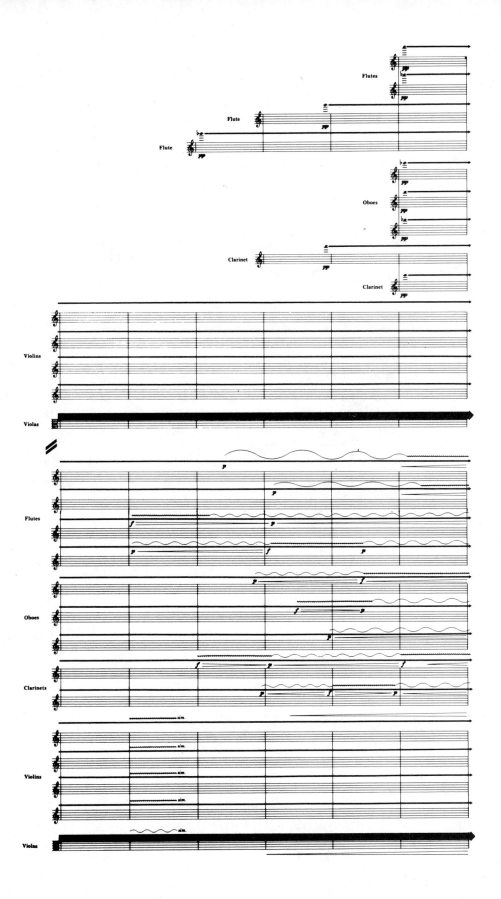

Music Notation...
The Journey that Took
1200 Years

The **oral tradition** began with the origin of music. This tradition, which you participated in when studying Chapter 1, continues today as an important way of sharing songs with each other and of passing them on from one generation to the next.

The **written tradition** began as musicians realized that they needed a way of representing musical sounds so that music could be learned more accurately. The earliest notation that was devised would not have helped you learn a new song. It would, however, have helped you recall a song you already knew. This early notation consisted mostly of signs that stood for individual sounds and groups of sounds. These signs did not represent an exact pitch, nor did they indicate the relative length of individual sounds. The signs for notes were called **neumes.**

- Here is a familiar song as it might have looked had it been written around the year 800 A.D. Can you recognize it?

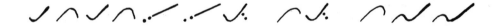

Just as you discovered that more information is needed if one is to reproduce a musical pattern accurately, the performers of a thousand years ago came to the same conclusion. However, it took nearly 800 years to develop the symbols that make our present notational system so useful! The process was so lengthy because new signs and symbols were invented only as musicians felt the need for them.

More precise ways to represent exact pitches came first. Lines were added to the notation, and each was given a letter name. Pitches that occurred between the lines were to be performed in relation to these pitches.

- Can you see some problems that might have occurred? Try performing this song. Do you recognize it?

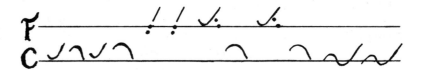

It was many years before the five-line **staff** as we know it today was commonly used. Around 1200, you might have seen this kind of pitch notation on a four-line staff. The symbol at the beginning shows the placement of C.

- Can you name the other pitches and sing the melody in rhythm? Do you recognize it?

The use of letters at the beginning of the staff gradually became standardized until today two letters are used most frequently. We call them **clefs.**

These became this.   These became this.

The trend toward a more precise notation of rhythm came somewhat later. Gradually, people realized that the length of a note could be indicated by its relation to the notes surrounding it.

- Try reading a rhythm written as it might have been written 500 years ago. Can you rewrite it in our notation?

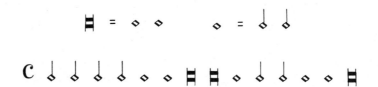

The clue to the change in relationships is the sign at the beginning of the rhythm. These signs eventually were replaced by our **meter signatures.** Later, the **bar line** was added. Bar lines help the performer see notes in groups, making the rhythm easier to read. The bar line has been in use for less than 400 years.

Here is a melody that is probably unfamiliar to you. Try singing it from each of the three staffs.

- This is how it might have looked around 1200 A.D.

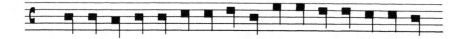

- In the fifteenth century, the melody might have looked like this.

- By the sixteenth century, when this melody was written, the same melody probably looked something like this.

On the next page, this same melody is written in the notation system used today. Which of the four systems seems to be easiest? What information is given in the system used today that you found hard to determine in the other examples?

Even though it has taken 1200 years for notation to come this far, the journey is not over. As you discovered at the beginning of this chapter, composers are still developing ways of representing their musical ideas.

TALLIS' CANON

Words by Joseph Addison

Music by Thomas Tallis

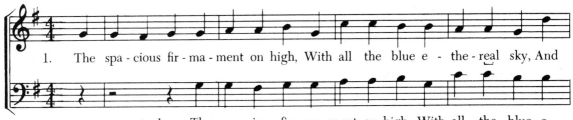

1. The spa-cious fir-ma-ment on high, With all the blue e - the-real sky, And

1. The spa-cious fir-ma-ment on high, With all the blue e -

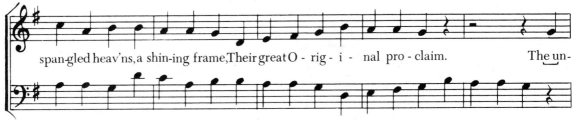

span-gled heav'ns, a shin-ing frame, Their great O - rig - i - nal pro-claim. The un-

the- real sky, And span-gled heav'ns, a shin-ing frame, Their great O - rig - i - nal pro-claim.

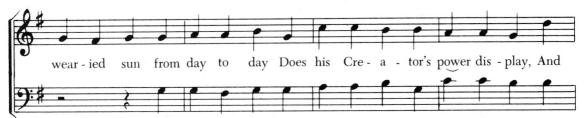

wear-ied sun from day to day Does his Cre - a - tor's power dis - play, And

The un - wear-ied sun from day to day Does his Cre - a - tor's

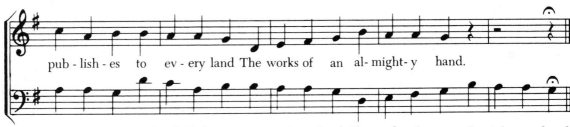

pub - lish - es to ev - ery land The works of an al - might-y hand.

power dis-play, And pub-lish-es to ev - ery land The works of an al- might-y hand.

2. Soon as the evening shades prevail
   The moon takes up the wondrous
      tale,
   And nightly to the listening earth
   Repeats the story of her birth;
   Whilst all the stars that round her
      burn,
   And all the planets in their turn,
   Confirm the tidings, as they roll,
   And spread the truth from pole to
      pole.

3. What though in solemn silence, all
   Move round the dark terrestrial ball;
   What though nor real voice nor sound
   Amid their radiant orbs be found;
   In reason's ear they all rejoice,
   And utter forth a glorious voice;
   For ever singing as they shine,
   "The hand that made us is divine."

Read Rhythm: Start with the Shortest Sound

Learn the rhythm of this song by adding short sounds together.

Follow the musical "plus" sign: ⌣

Chant the words in relation to the series of short sounds.
Tap *all* of the short sounds while you chant the rhythm of the words.

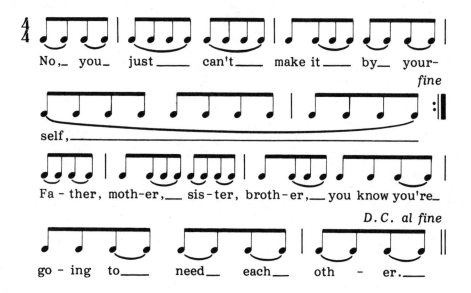

Compare the way the short sounds were added together with the rhythmic notation of the song, as written on page 29.

Read Melody: Start with the Tonal Center

TUNE-UP

1	3	5	1'	5	3	1	5,	1
E	G#	B	E'	B	G#	E	B,	E

YOU JUST CAN'T MAKE IT BY YOURSELF

Words and Music by Barbara Dane

Baritones may add a bass part by singing the root of the chords shown above the melodic notation.

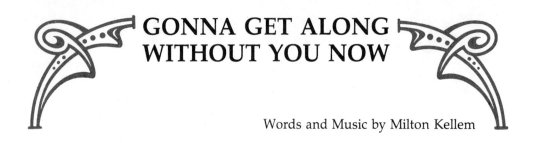

GONNA GET ALONG WITHOUT YOU NOW

Words and Music by Milton Kellem

Figure out the rhythm of the melody.

- Start with the shortest sound.
- Determine the length of other notes by adding short sounds together.

Figure out the melody.

- Start with the tonal center: 1
- Sing pitches of the I chord: 1-3-5
- Determine the sound of other pitches in relation to these chordal pitches.

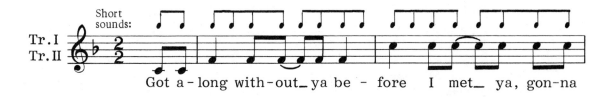

Copyright © 1952 Bibo Music Publishers. Copyright renewed. International copyright secured. All rights reserved. Used by permission.

twice as cute— 'cause ya did-n't love me an-y-how.— You

ran a-round— with ev-'ry girl in town— and ya nev-er cared—if it

got me down.— You had me wor-ried, al-ways on my guard,— But ya

laughed at me— 'cause I tried too hard. Boom-Boom, Boom-

Boom, Gon-na get a-long with-out ya now.— Boom-Boom, Boom-

Boom, Gon-na get a-long with-out ya now.—

When you have learned the rhythm and the melody, listen to the arrangement on the recording.

Which voices should sing the harmony part?

Sounds Exist in Time

We sense the passing of time by the ticking of the clock.
We sense the passing of musical time by movement of musical sounds.
Listen to music. Count the passage of time.

Look at written music for information about counting musical time.

The **meter signature** gives one way to count:

- Look at the upper number. ⟶ It tells you to count in groups.

$$\frac{6}{8}$$

- Look at the lower number. ⟶ It identifies the note that lasts for one count.

Look beyond the **meter signature** for other information:

Bar lines group notes into **measures.**

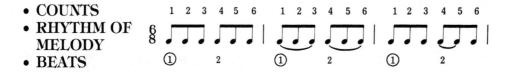

- COUNTS
- RHYTHM OF MELODY
- BEATS

Within each **measure,** notes may again be grouped to show their relation to the **underlying beat.**

BRETHREN IN PEACE TOGETHER

Paraphrase of Psalm 133:1   Jewish Folk Song

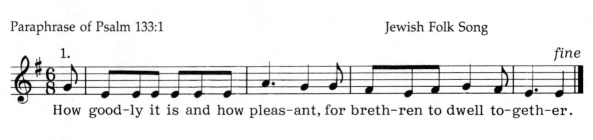

How good-ly it is and how pleas-ant, for breth-ren to dwell to-geth-er.

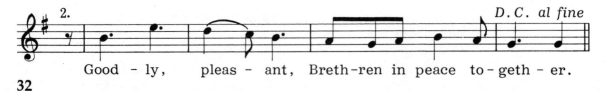

Good - ly,   pleas - ant,   Breth-ren in peace to-geth - er.

Sounds Exist in Space

We sense the rhythmic movement of music through time. We sense its melodic movement through space. Listen to "Brethren in Peace Together." Draw its melodic movement.

Numbers measure rhythmic movement through time. Numbers also measure the distance between pitches in a melody. In written music, the placement of notes on a staff helps us measure the distance between pitches in relation to the **tonal center.**

To begin measuring melodic movement, first locate the **tonal center.** Look at the **key signature** and beyond to the melody. Determine the pitches around which the melody moves.

A song with this **key signature** might center around

these pitches: these pitches:

Key of G Major   **Key of E minor**

↑   ↑

TONAL CENTER   TONAL CENTER

Look at "Brethren in Peace Together." Which pitch is the **tonal center?**

Practice singing each pitch in the **E minor scale** in relation to the tonal center.

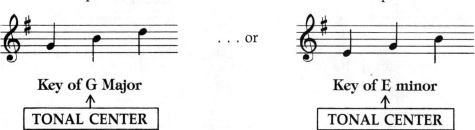

Use this musical knowledge to learn the song.
Add a **drone** accompaniment on a **bass** instrument:

GOIN' DOWN TO TOWN

American Folk Song

Look at the **meter signature** of this song.
How will the rhythm be counted?
In this song, are **beats** and **counts** the same or different?

- COUNTS
- RHYTHM OF MELODY
- BEATS

We could change the meter signature and count this rhythm
in a different way. Has the way the beats are grouped been
changed?

- COUNTS
- RHYTHM OF MELODY
- BEATS

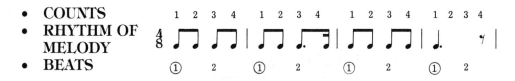

Use one of these ways of counting and learn the rhythm
of the melody.

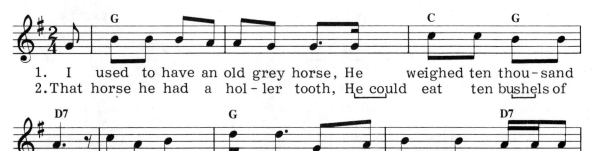

1. I used to have an old grey horse, He weighed ten thou-sand
2. That horse he had a hol-ler tooth, He could eat ten bushels of

pounds, Ev-'ry tooth in his head was eight - een in-ches a-
corn, Ev-'ry time he o-pened his mouth, Two bushels and a half were

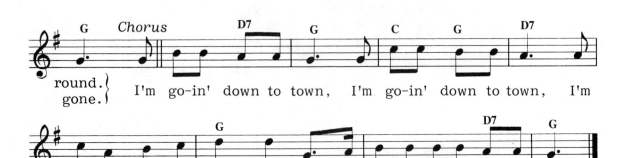

round.
gone. I'm go-in' down to town, I'm go-in' down to town, I'm

go-in' down to Lynch-burg town, To car-ry my to-bac-co down.

"Goin' Down to Town" has the same **key signature** as "Brethren in Peace Together."

- Review the discussion on page 32.
- Then look at the notation of "Goin' Down to Town."
- What is its **tonal center?**

Prepare for reading the melody of the song. Practice singing pitches of the **G major** scale in relation to the **tonal center.**

Improvise a skiffle band accompaniment for this song.

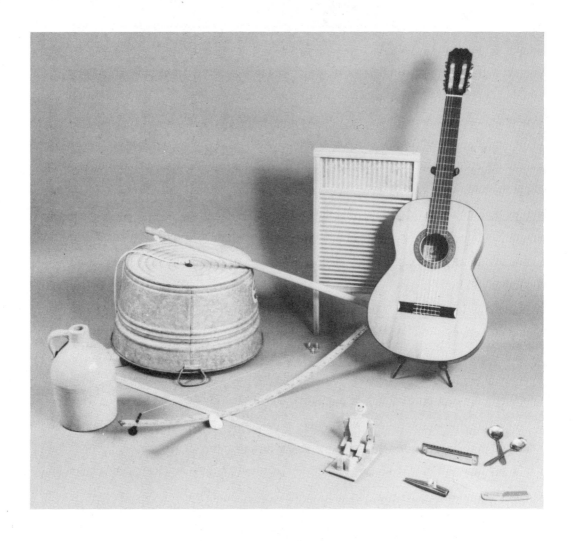

Learn to play these instruments by turning to page 114.

Looking Beyond

Listen to "Gymnopédie No. 3" by Erik Satie and "Waltz" from *Les Patineurs* by Giacomo Meyerbeer.

- How do you sense the rhythmic movement of each example?
- Count softly to yourself as you listen to each piece of music.
- Call each heavy beat **"1."**

Which of these patterns matches the way you counted the rhythmic movement?

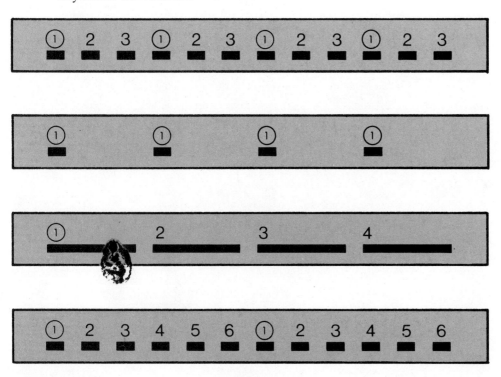

You may have counted the two musical examples in different ways because of differences in the **performance style** of the two compositions.

- **tempo**
- **nature of the accompaniment**
- **rhythm of the melody**
- **relationship between heavy and light beats**

Compare the two scores on page 37.
Notice that the **meter signatures** are the same.

In order to make decisions about appropriate performance style, the players had to look beyond the meter signature.

GYMNOPÉDIE NO. 3

by Erik Satie

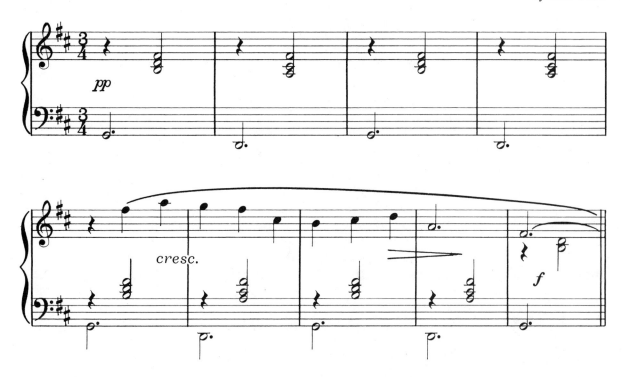

WALTZ

from "Les Patineurs"
(excerpt)

by Giacomo Meyerbeer

KID STUFF

Arranged by Emily Bedient   Traditional

Learn to perform "Kid Stuff" and "William Goat" (page 40). The **meter signatures** of both songs tells you to count in threes. To decide the appropriate rhythmic style of each song, you will need to "look beyond."
Consider:

- **tempo**
- **nature of accompaniment**
- **rhythm of the melody**
- **the beats which should be most strongly stressed**

When you have determined the rhythmic style of "Kid Stuff," learn to sing this arrangement. To begin, you will need to look beyond the **key signature** to determine the **tonal center.**

• Around which of these groups of pitches does the melody move?

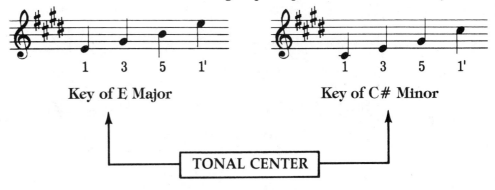

Just as the melody of a song centers around certain pitches, so does its harmony:

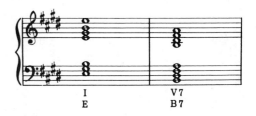

• Choose the part you are going to sing.
• Study the pitches. ·
• Can you tell when you will be singing pitches of the I chord? the V^7 chord?

WILLIAM GOAT

Words Anonymous

American Folk Melody
Arranged by B. A.

Will you use the same rhythmic style for "William Goat" that you used for "Kid Stuff"? Will the groupings of threes flow in the same way or a different way? Look at the **meter signature** and beyond to make your decision. This song is in the same **key** as "Kid Stuff." Follow the same procedures to learn this arrangement.

Tr. II — Mar - y had a Will - iam Goat, Will - iam Goat, Will - iam Goat,

Tr. I — Nay nay nay nay nay nay nay nay

C.V. — Nay nay nay nay nay nay nay nay

Bar. — Nay nay nay nay nay nay nay nay

Mar - y had a Will - iam Goat and he was lined with zinc.

nay nay nay nay nay nay nay.

nay nay nay nay nay nay nay.

nay nay nay nay nay nay nay.

HOCHZEITSMARSCH

from *Ein Sommernachtstraum*

by Felix Mendelssohn

Listen to this ceremonial march.
Count softly to yourself as you listen.
Which one of these patterns matches the rhythmic
movement of what you hear?

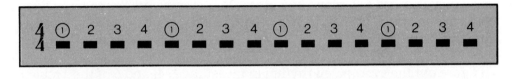

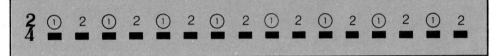

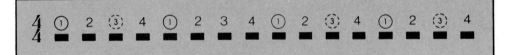

Some of you may have counted the music in twos.
What does the meter signature of the opening phrase suggest?

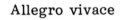

Allegro vivace

Why do you suppose some of you may have sensed this
music in twos? Were it counted this way, every other beat
would be felt as equally heavy:

Listen again. Can you sense that it moves more like this?

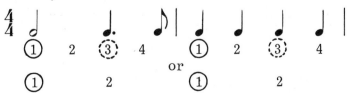

OH BE JOYFUL

from *Gaudeamus Hodie* (Let Us Rejoice Today)

Words and Music by Natalie Sleeth

This song also has a $\frac{4}{4}$ **meter signature.** Will it move in the same way as "Hochzeitsmarsch"? What do you need to think about to make your decision and learn the rhythm?

To figure out the **syncopated** rhythm in measures 2, 4, and 6 of the Treble **I** part, try counting in eights.

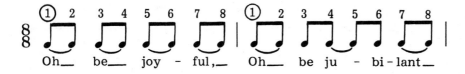

The tonal center of this song is C.
Tune up with the **C major scale:**

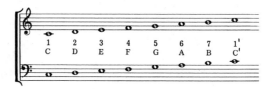

Learn your part by singing it with scale numbers. Measure each pitch in relation to its distance from the tonal center, **1.**

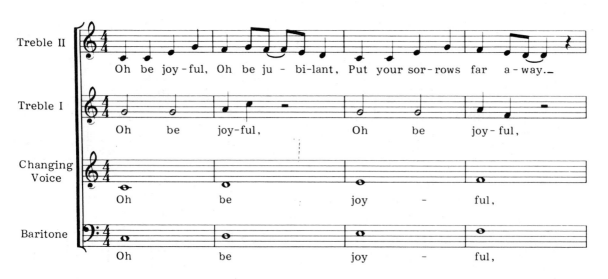

Copyright © 1972 by Carl Fischer, Inc., New York, N.Y. International copyright secured. All rights reserved. Reprinted by permission of the publisher.

42

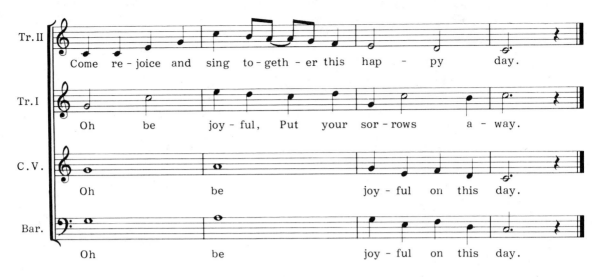

When learning your parts for this song, did you discover that the **Changing Voice** and **Baritone** parts have the same melody? They do not look the same on the staff because . . .

one is written in the **Treble** or **G Clef**

and the other is in the **Bass** or **F Clef**

Both parts sing the same scale steps one octave (eight steps) apart. To determine letter names for the pitches of these two **clefs,** remember that the note between the clefs is Middle C.

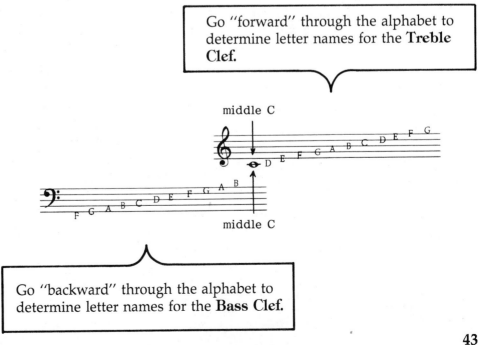

Go "forward" through the alphabet to determine letter names for the **Treble Clef.**

middle C

middle C

Go "backward" through the alphabet to determine letter names for the **Bass Clef.**

More Help from the Meter Signature

Perform the following three rhythms. Apply the information supplied by the **meter signature.**

The **upper number** helps you know:	The **lower number** helps you determine:
• how to count the rhythmic movement of a song.	• the note that lasts one count; • relationship of other notes to one count.

In what ways does the notation for these three patterns look the same? different? Did the rhythms sound the same? different? Why?

THIS TRAIN

American Folk Song

Learn to sing "This Train" by reading the **treble clef.** Baritones will need to sing an octave (**8va**) lower.

1. This train is bound for glo-ry, this train!__
2. This train don't pull no ex-tras, this train!__

This train is bound for glo-ry, this train!__
This train don't pull no ex-tras, this train!__

This train is bound for glo - ry,
This train don't pull no ex - tras,

D.C. al fine

Don't ride noth - in' but the good and ho - ly.
Don't pull noth - in' but the mid - night spe - cial.

Here are **ostinati** that may be performed as an accompaniment to "This Train."

Each pattern appears twice—once in the **treble clef** and once in the **bass clef.**

- Match each pair of patterns. Choose one in your voice range.
- Each **ostinato** begins on one of the pitches of the **I chord.**
- On which pitch does yours begin? the root? the third? the fifth?
- Repeat your pattern over and over while others sing the melody.

Whoo, whoo,___ whoo
Whoo, whoo,___ whoo
Whoo, whoo,___ whoo
Whoo, whoo,___ whoo
Whoo, whoo,___ whoo
Whoo, whoo,___ whoo

Develop an arrangement for "This Train." Plan
    an **introduction,**
    an **interlude,** and
    a **coda**
using some of the **ostinati.**

Try using instruments instead of voices for some of the accompaniment parts.

Add this rhythm part.
Will you use it throughout?

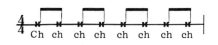

Ch ch ch ch ch ch ch ch

Ostinato parts by Jeri Yoffee Silvester.
Used by permission.

45

Read Melody in a Major Tonality

Music is easier to read and sing if you can sense the relationship of the pitches to each other. To find this out, you need to know the **tonal center** of the melody and the **scale** on which it is based.

Look at "It Ain't Gonna Rain" on page 47. It appears in four different **keys**—that is, with four different **tonal centers**.

Learn the melody in the **key** that is best for your voice range. First, discover the **tonal center** and the **scale**. To do this, you will need to prepare a **Chromatic Scale Ruler** and a **Major Scale Finder.**

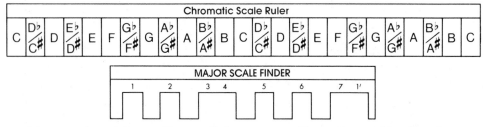

How to Use the Chromatic Scale Ruler and Major Scale Finder

1. Locate the **tonal center** of the melody. Do this by finding the note around which the song seems to center. It is often the last note of the song.

2. Locate each *different* pitch in the song.

3. Starting with the **tonal center,** circle all the pitches you have located on your Chromatic Scale Ruler. Mark them in order, from low to high.

4. Place the Major Scale Finder over your Chromatic Scale Ruler so that the **tonal center** appears in the first cutout of the Finder.

Self-Check 1: Each pitch you circled on your Chromatic Scale Ruler should now show in the cutouts of the Major Scale Finder.

Self-Check 2: Apply the appropriate rule as follows:

- **Sharps**—The last sharp to the right is the seventh step of the scale. Count down lines and spaces to find "1."

- **Flats**—The last flat to the right is the fourth step of the scale. Count down lines and spaces to find "1."

When you count down, you should end on the line or space that you identified as the tonal center in Step 1.

IT AIN'T GONNA RAIN

Wendell Woods Hall

Have you identified the tonal center and the major scale pitches for each version of this song by following the steps on page 46? Play the scales on resonator bells or xylophone. Do they sound right?

Compare the four versions of "It Ain't Gonna Rain."
What is the same? What is different?

Read Melodies in Different Tonalities

"It Ain't Gonna Rain" appears four times on page 47. Each version has a different **key signature,** but is based on the same **major tonality.**

The songs on pages 48–52 all have the same **key signature,** but are based on **different tonalities.**

Determine the tonality of each song. To begin you will need:

- your **Chromatic Scale Ruler;**
- **Scale Finders** for several different scales.

Look at the song "The Cruel War" on page 49. First, follow steps 1, 2, and 3 on page 46. Then continue with these steps:

4. Experiment with each **Scale Finder.** Place them, one at a time, over the **Chromatic Scale Ruler** until you find the scale that matches the pitches you circled.

5. When you have located the correct scale, establish tonality by playing and singing the scale. Then learn the song after you have determined its rhythm.

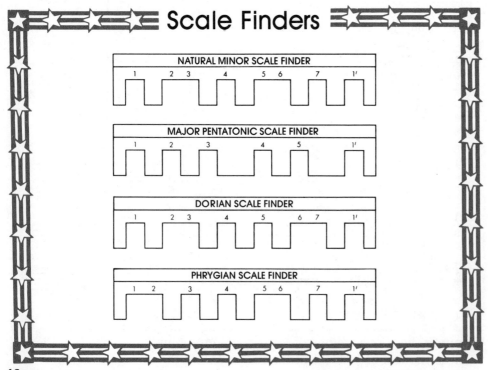

Scale Finders

NATURAL MINOR SCALE FINDER
1   2 3   4   5 6   7   1'

MAJOR PENTATONIC SCALE FINDER
1   2   3   4   5   1'

DORIAN SCALE FINDER
1   2 3   4   5   6 7   1'

PHRYGIAN SCALE FINDER
1 2   3   4   5 6   7   1'

THE CRUEL WAR

Words and Music by Paul Stookey and Peter Yarrow

1. The cruel war is rag - ing and John - ny has to
2. I'll go to your cap - tain, get down___ on my
3. Ten thou - sand gold gui - neas, it grieves___ my heart

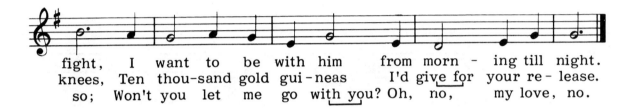

fight, I want to be with him from morn - ing till night.
knees, Ten thou-sand gold gui - neas I'd give for your re - lease.
so; Won't you let me go with you? Oh, no, my love, no.

4. Tomorrow is Sunday and Monday is the day
   Your captain calls for you, and you must obey.

5. Your captain calls for you, it grieves my heart so,
   Won't you let me go with you? — Oh, no, my love, no.

6. I'll pull back my hair, men's clothes I'll put on,
   I'll pass for your comrade as we march along.

7. I'll pass for your comrade and none will ever guess,
   Won't you let me go with you? — Yes, my love, yes.

Chords based on other scales may be used to accompany pentatonic melodies. Use these chords from the major scale as an accompaniment to "The Cruel War." **Treble I's** and **Baritones** may take turns singing the verses.

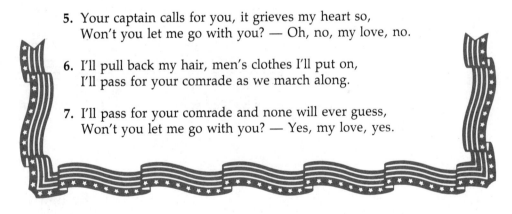

GET THY BEARINGS

Words and Music by Donovan Leitch

Determine the scale used in this song. When you name the pitches, be sure to add ♯ (sharp) or ♭ (flat) after the letter name when appropriate. To find out where sharps and flats occur, you need to watch for:

- the **key signature;**
- **accidentals:** sharps ♯ , flats ♭ , and naturals ♮ in front of notes in the melody.

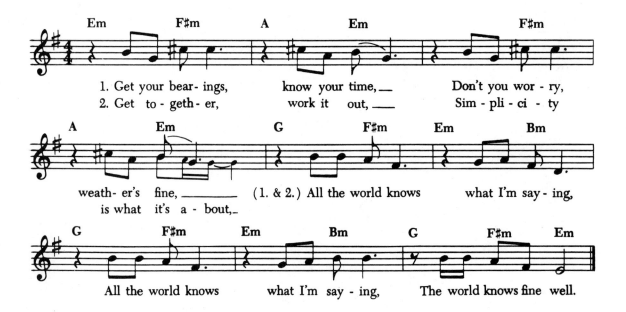

The range of this song may be uncomfortable for some voices. You can improvise your own harmonizing part for melodies if you know how to read chord symbols and figure out the pitches that belong to each chord.

Follow the steps on page 60 to add a harmony part for "Get Thy Bearings."

Add a percussion accompaniment:

Copyright © 1968 by Donovan (Music) Ltd. Sole selling agent Peer International Corporation. Used by permission.

WAYFARIN' STRANGER

Adapted and Arranged by Buryl Red

American Folk Song

Follow the steps on page 48.

- Look at both the melody and harmony as you list the pitches.
- You will discover both B♮ and B♭.
- You will need to build two scales. First, use only B♮ in your scale. Then build it again using B♭.

What differences do you notice in the form of the scales? Did you need two different **Scale Finders?**

Copyright © 1971 by Generic Music. All rights reserved. Used by permission.

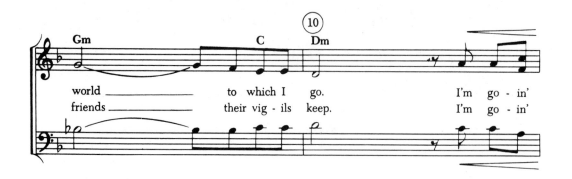

world _____ to which I go. I'm go - in'
friends _____ their vig - ils keep. I'm go - in'

there _____ to see my fa - ther, I'm go - in'
there _____ to see my moth - er; She said she'd

there _____ no more to roam, I'm just a -
meet _____ me when I come. I'm on - ly

go - in' o - ver Jor - dan, I'm just a -
go - in' o - ver Jor - dan, I'm on - ly

go - in'__ o - ver home.
go - in'__ o - ver

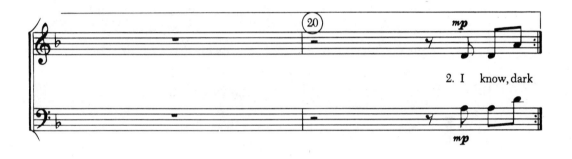

2. I know, dark

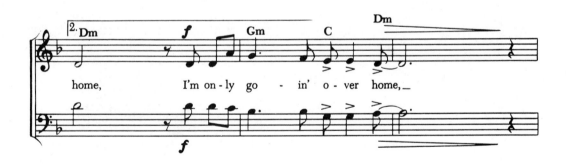

home, I'm on - ly go - in' o - ver home,__

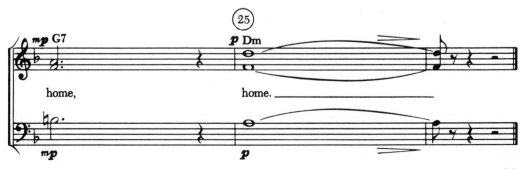

home, home._____

Changing from Measure to Measure

WATER

Words by Hilda Conkling   Music by Donald Erb

Do these meter signatures direct you to count in relation to the underlying beat or to a shorter unit of sound?

Describe the relationship of notes and rests to the **beats;** to the **counts.**

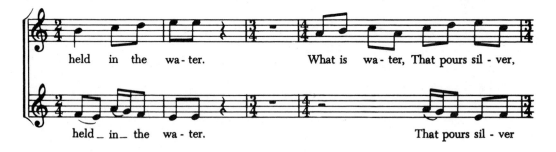

Changing with the Measure

HUAPANGO

Mexican Folk Dance

Listen to this dance from Mexico. How do you sense the grouping of beats? Is it always the same? Look at the rhythm of the first two phrases. How would you count it? How do the beats seem to be grouped within each measure? What meter signature would you place at the beginning?

Would you use changing meter signatures as in "Water" on page 54?

Did you sense the shifting between groupings of the beats in twos and threes? This rhythmic style is typical of many Latin-American songs and dances.

Taffeta Tigers

by B.A.

Perform this chant by counting in fives. Chant the words.
Clap every count. Stamp beats.

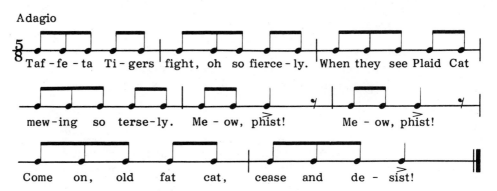

Adagio

Taf - fe - ta Ti - gers fight, oh so fierce - ly. When they see Plaid Cat

mew - ing so terse - ly. Me - ow, phist! Me - ow, phist!

Come on, old fat cat, cease and de - sist!

Can you make up a chant that would be counted in sevens? eights?
How will you group the beats within the measures?

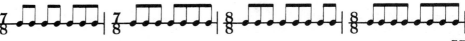

BILLY THE KID

(excerpt)

by Aaron Copland

Aaron Copland composed "Billy the Kid" for a ballet based on the life of Brooklyn-born William Bonney—the infamous "Billy the Kid." This excerpt is from a concert suite arranged by the composer from the original dance score.

Listen to the ways Copland makes use of a variety of meters and rhythmic styles to convey the jaunty mood of a western pioneer town.

1 A "whistlin' tune" begins the scene. This melody is counted in twos.

Other woodwinds echo fragments.
Portions of the theme are repeated, alternating with a fragment of "Get Along Little Dogies."

2 Violas, cellos, bassoons, and horns take over the "Dogie" theme; these are joined by other winds and strings. Listen for the dissonance created by instruments playing a half-step apart on long tones.

3 The first theme returns, now accompanied by a steady "oom-pah, oom-pah" pattern in the strings.

4 Listen as the "oom-pah, oom-pah" accompaniment shifts to "oom-pah-pah, oom-pah-pah" while the melody continues in twos. This is accomplished by changing note groupings and accents within the measure, not by changing meter signatures.

5 By accenting different tones in the theme, the melody shifts between threes and fours. The cowboy tune takes on a Spanish flair.

6

A gradual decrescendo leads into a brief but vigorous interlude which prepares the way for a new theme.

Lower strings and brass set the feeling of the beat moving in fours. Over this, strings introduce another melodic idea, later punctuated by trumpet.

7

Trombones introduce "Get Along Little Dogies" in its most recognizable form. Notice that altered groupings within the measure have changed the rhythmic style once more!

The string theme returns, bringing the rhythmic movement back to a steady four.

8

Oboe and trumpet introduce "Get Along Little Dogies" as originally stated in twos. Listen for the return of the first theme played by piccolo, now in rhythmic **diminution.**

9 Legato fragments in the brass prepare us for another melodic idea and a new meter. Notice how the notes are now grouped within the measure.

10 The oboe momentarily takes over the lead, quickly resumed by the trumpet.

11 Without warning, the strings introduce "Good-bye, Old Paint" in threes.

But this is not a simple three. Notice that the melody, played by the oboes, and accompaniment, played by the clarinets, move in contrast to each other, but both still move in threes.

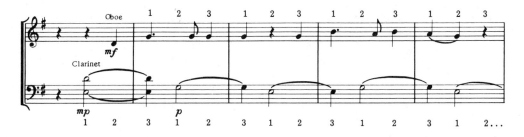

The wistful melody continues over the same style of accompaniment, passed back and forth between strings and oboe.

12 The trumpet, still stating the same theme, introduces a more dramatic mood. The texture thickens as more instruments join in, building to the sustained tones which end this section of the ballet.

Improvise a Harmonizing Part

Add your own harmonization to "Five Hundred Miles."

You will need:

- a Chord Chart
- three Chord Finders
- a Chromatic Scale Ruler
- staff paper
- pencil

Follow these steps to discover the pitch names for each chord:

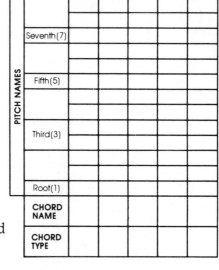

1. Write the name of each different chord used in the accompaniment in the **chord name** row of your chart.

2. Write the type of chord in the **chord type** row. The chord type is identified by its symbol:
   - **F** = major triad
   - **Fm** = minor triad
   - **F7** = dominant seventh

3. Locate the appropriate Chord Finder. Place it over the Chromatic Ruler so that the root shows in the cutout marked "Root" (1).

4. Copy the names of all the pitches appearing in the Chord Finder cutouts into the correct boxes above the chord name. Leave empty boxes to indicate skipped pitches.

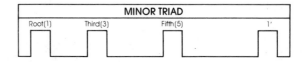

FIVE HUNDRED MILES

Words and Music by Hedy West

Add a singable part which harmonizes with the melody.

1. On blank staff paper, mark off each measure of the song with bar lines. Then write the chord symbols above the staff, one for each measure.

2. Decide on a rhythm for your harmony part.
   - Will you sing the same words and rhythm as the melody?
   - Will you sing in a contrasting rhythm to the melody?
   - Will you perform the same rhythm throughout?

3. Decide on the melodic patterns you will use. To do this, choose pitches that:
   - belong to the chord harmonizing the appropriate measure.
   - move easily from one pitch to the next. Avoid big skips.
   - pass between chord tones. Use these pitches on unaccented beats.

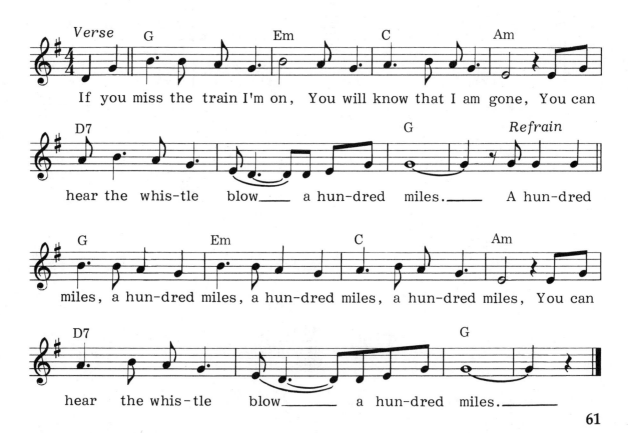

Verse
G   Em   C   Am
If you miss the train I'm on, You will know that I am gone, You can

D7   G   Refrain
hear the whis-tle blow___ a hun-dred miles.___ A hun-dred

G   Em   C   Am
miles, a hun-dred miles, a hun-dred miles, a hun-dred miles, You can

D7   G
hear the whis-tle blow___ a hun-dred miles.___

TURN AROUND, LOOK AT ME

Arranged by Fred Bock

Words and Music by Jerry Capehart

Would the rhythm of your part be easier to read if it had been written with this meter signature?

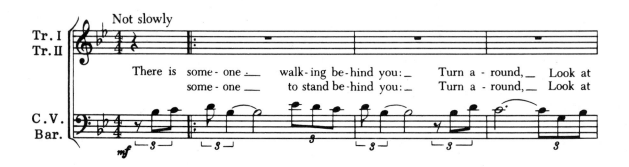

Copyright © 1961 by Viva Music Co. All rights reserved. Used by permission.

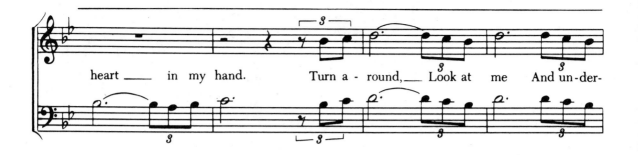

heart _____ in my hand. Turn a - round,_ Look at me And un-der-

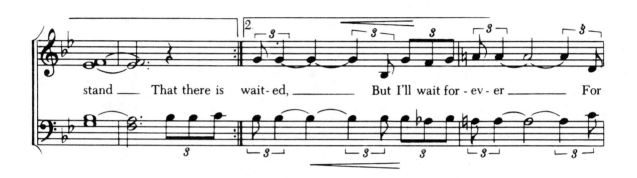

stand _____ That there is wait-ed, _____ But I'll wait for - ev - er _____ For

you to come to me. Look at some-one _ who real - ly loves you: _ Turn a-

round, Turn a - round, Look _ at me. _____

Turn a - round, Turn and look _ at me. _____

The Rhythms of Rock and Jazz

KATHY'S COOKIN'

by Tom Ferguson

Listen to two performances of the same melody. One is in rock style; the other is jazz. What differences do you notice?

- Pay particular attention to the rhythmic style of the two performances.
- As you listen again, study the designs below.
- Which best shows the movement you sensed when listening to the first example? the second?

As you listen to both performances again, accompany them with these two patterns. Try both patterns with each example. Which best fits the rock version? the jazz?

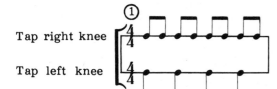 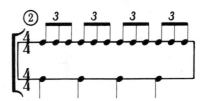

The first performance was in rock style.
Like many rock arrangements, it was built upon a short-note relationship of two-to-the-beat, such as:

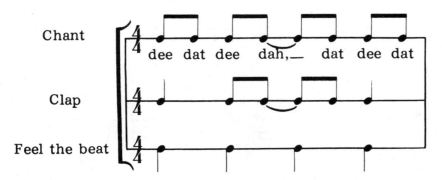

Listen again to the rock version of "Kathy's Cookin'." Perform along with the recording according to this plan:

- **Introduction**—listen.
- **A Section**—perform the pattern at the bottom of page 64.
- **B Section**—improvise.
- **Interlude I**—listen (two measures).
- **B Section**—improvise.
- **Interlude I**—listen (two measures).
- **B Section**—improvise.
- **Interlude II**—listen.
- **A Section**—perform the pattern at the bottom of page 64.

Listen and perform again. This time, improvise a melody during the **B Section.** Use either set of pitches:

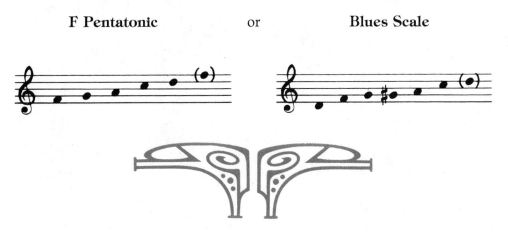

F Pentatonic   or   **Blues Scale**

Now listen to the jazz version of "Kathy's Cookin'." Jazz is often based on a short-note relationship of three-to-the-beat, as shown by this pattern:

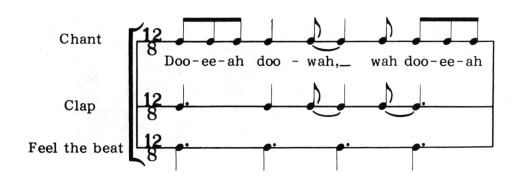

Perform along with the jazz version; follow the same plan you used when accompanying the rock version. This time use the chant based on threes during the **A Section.**

VARIATIONS ON AMERICA

Arranged by William Schuman   Music by Charles Ives

"Variations on America" was composed in 1891 by sixteen-year-old Charles Ives. He played it in an organ concert on the Fourth of July.

Follow this music map of Ives' piece as arranged by the American composer, William Schuman. Notice ways that rhythmic, melodic, and harmonic changes affect the style.

This color code will help you identify instruments:

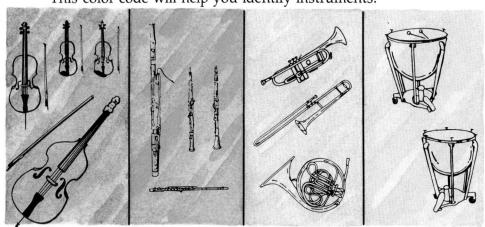

1 INTRODUCTION

2 THEME   How quickly can you identify this familiar song?

3 VARIATION 1

Chromatic Ornaments

Theme

66

4 VARIATION 2

Theme
New harmonics in accompaniment

5 INTERLUDE   a **polytonal canon**

6 VARIATION 3   change in grouping of beats and rhythm of melody

7 VARIATION 4   a polonaise

Theme

8 INTERLUDE   **polytonal** chords leading to . . .

9 VARIATION 5   an imitation of marching band music

Theme

Theme repeated

10 CONCLUSION   Fragments of the theme build to a powerful climax. Can you still hear the theme?

Unit 11

THE WHOLE EARTH'S MUSIC

A Journey Through Time and Space

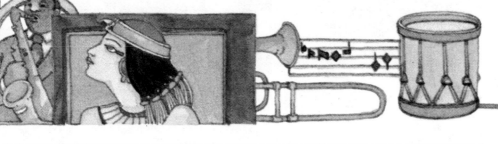

CHART 9: Commitment to Musical Learning (3)	
In this section you will have an opportunity to . . .	
hear and perform vocal and instrumental music of various cultures	identify and describe distinctive vocal characteristics
make and play your own instruments	identify and categorize characteristics of instrumental sounds

- Which of these can you now do independently?
- In which of these areas will you commit yourself to becoming more independent?

Crossing the Barriers of Land and Sea

By listening to samples of the whole earth's music, we can instantly travel over the vast distances of our great world.

We can cross oceans to visit tribal villages hidden from visitors . . . we can secretly enter the ritual grounds where people celebrate their age-old festivals and ceremonies. We can hear workers singing in the fields . . . shepherds singing in distant mountains . . . sailors' chanteys roaring above a sea we have never seen.

The music of the whole earth's people is a vital part of the history of our world. For wherever people settle, they leave behind a **living** music that says

THIS IS HOW WE THINK!
THIS IS WHAT WE LOVE!
THIS IS WHAT WE BELIEVE IN!
THIS IS HOW WE EXPRESS WHO WE ARE!

Expression through singing, dancing, and playing is a people's musical "thumbprint"—the clue that says

I WAS HERE!
REMEMBER ME!

Five Vocal Characteristics

Vocal sounds may seem pleasing or displeasing to you because of your past experience. The vocal characteristics of singers are influenced by their past experience.

The way a person sings involves many vocal characteristics. Five of these are especially important. Think about these basic characteristics and how YOU might change your own vocal sound!

Quality

Experiment: Sing "ah" with relaxed facial and neck muscles. Make the sound as **rich** and open as you can. Then switch to "ee," tightening your singing muscles. Make the sound as tense and **thin** as you can. Even sing through your nose! Now use one of these qualities to sing a familiar song.

Performance Style

Experiment: Sing the same familiar song in a smooth, flowing *legato* way. Then repeat it in a disconnected, choppy *staccato* manner.

Expression

Experiment: Sing the same song in a very flat, colorless way, with almost no changes in vocal quality or dynamics. Repeat the song, this time exploring a wide variety of qualities and dynamics.

Register

Experiment: Sing a song that includes pitches in your middle register. Sing it again in a very high register. Sing it once again in a very low register. Listen to yourself! Does a change of register affect the vocal color?

Tremolo

Experiment: Sing a long, steady "ah" in your middle register. Then gradually fluctuate the sound slightly above and below the initial steady pitch . . . first, a little . . . then a great deal. Now sing the same song using tremolo.

Listen again to the vocal sounds you heard on page 69. Describe the vocal characteristics of each voice by filling in one "Five Vocal Characteristics" Chart for each singer. As you make your decisions, place an X somewhere along each line for each characteristic. Did you and your classmates make the same decisions?

CHART 10: Five Vocal Characteristics

Title . . . .   **Country** . . . .

Quality	thin, nasal				rich, open
	1	2	3	4	5

Performance Style	choppy				flowing
	1	2	3	4	5

Expression	limited				widely varied
	1	2	3	4	5

Register	very high				very low
	1	2	3	4	5

Tremolo	little				much
	1	2	3	4	5

71

The Whole Earth Sings

- OLDEST RABBIT SONG

  Sioux Indian

- TROUBLE IN MIND

  (excerpt)
  United States

- LA HUICHOLA

  Mexico

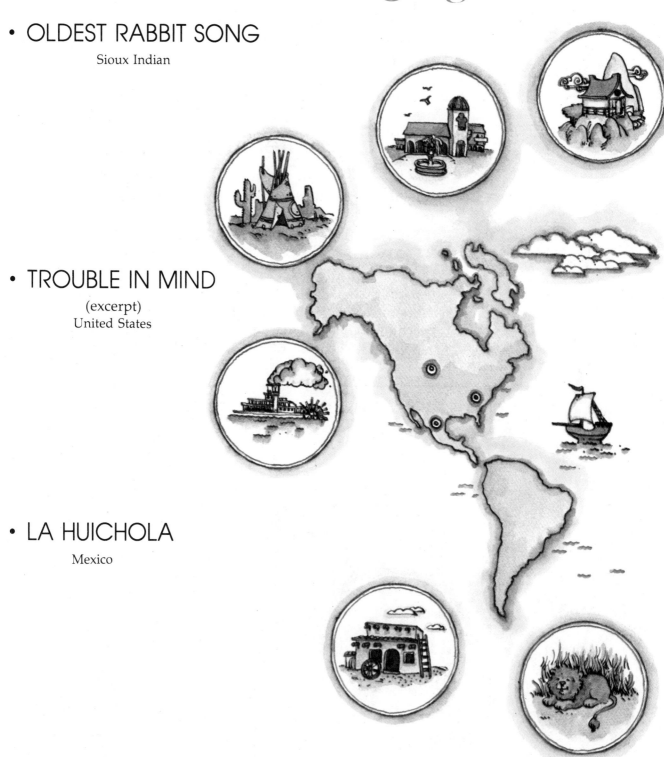

• SAETA

(excerpt)
Spain

• OGI NO MATO

(excerpt)
Japan

• RAGHUVĀRANANNU

(excerpt)
India

• HAKA KAMATE

New Zealand

• LULLABY

Central
African
Republic

- Listen to each singer.
- Fill in your chart of "Five Vocal
  Characteristics" for each voice.
- Discuss the different reasons why
  people sing.

73

BWANA, IBARIKI AFRIKA

African Folk Song

Listen to the recording.
Learn to perform this song in Swahili.
What vocal characteristics will you use?

With dignity

Bwa - na, i - ba - ri - ki Af - ri - ka, I - li - i - pa - te_____

ku - am - ka. Ma - om - bi ye to ya - si - ki - lel.

U - tu - ba - ri - ki. *Fine* U - je Ro - ho, U - je Ro - ho,_____

D.S. al fine
(with repeat)

U - je Ro - ho, U - je Ro - ho, U - ta - ja - ze.

Copyright © 1958 by Cooperative Recreation Service, Inc., Delaware, Ohio.

"Ramayana"—Hindu Epic

KETJAK CHORUS

The Monkey Chorus of Bali
(excerpt)

In Bali, as darkness falls, the "Monkey Chorus" enters the temple gate chanting *"ketjak, ketjak"* as they surround the stage. The dancers begin to dramatize an ancient story about Rama, the hero, and Rawana, King of the Demons. The Ketjak Chorus represents the army of monkeys who, led by Sugriwa their king, help Rama rescue his wife, Sita. While some singers continue the "Ketjak Chorus," others add a repetitive refrain.

Listen again!
- Mark your chart of "Five Vocal Characteristics" for the "Ketjak Chorus."
- Compare your decisions with those of your classmates.
- Discuss any other characteristics of this music that you think are important.

Plan a Performance!
- Choose several actors to dramatize the story about Rama and the monkey army.
- Choose some people to perform a repetitive refrain. They should make up a short melody and words.
- Everyone else takes the part of the "Ketjak Chorus." Listen to the recording once again. Concentrate on the vocal characteristics so that you will be able to imitate those sounds.
- Perform your own "Story of Rama."
- Discuss your own performance. Compare it with the recording.

HENRY MARTIN

Old English Ballad

1. There were ___ three broth - ers in mer - ry Scot - land, In mer - ry Scot - land there were three, ___ And they did cast lots which of them ___ should go, ___ should go, ___ should go ___ And ___ turn rob - ber all on the salt sea. ___

2. The lot ___ it fell up - on Hen - ry Mar - tin, The young - est of all ___ the three, ___ That he should turn rob - ber on all the salt sea, ___ salt sea, ___ salt sea ___ For to main - tain his two broth - ers and he. ___

3. He had not been sail - ing but a long win - ter's night, And part of a short win - ter's day, ___ Be - fore he es - pied a stout lof - ty ship, ___ a ship, ___ a ship ___ Come ___ a - rid - ing down on him straight - way. ___

4. "Hel - lo, ___ hel - lo," ___ cried Hen - ry Mar - tin, "What makes ___ you sail ___ so nigh?" ___ "I'm a rich mer - chant ship bound for fair Lon - don town, ___ fair Lon - don town, ___ Will ___ you please for to let me pass by?" ___

5. "Oh, no, oh, no," cried Henry Martin,
"That thing it never can be,
For I have turned robber on all the salt sea, salt sea, salt sea
For to maintain my two brothers and me."

6. "Then lower your topsail and bow down your mizzen,
Bow yourselves under my lee,
Or I shall give you a fast-flowing ball, a fast-flowing ball
And cast your dear bodies down in the salt sea."

"I Hear America Singing..."

The music of America is as diverse as its people—American Indian songs and dances, Afro-American blues-gospels, mountain and plains peoples' bluegrass, Hispanic music—all these and more make up true American music.

REELIN' AND ROCKIN'
by Chuck Berry

VIEJO SOCARRÓN
by Luis Grinan

I WALK THE LINE
by Johnny Cash

OH HAPPY DAY
by Edwin Hawkins

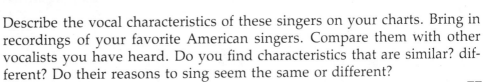

Describe the vocal characteristics of these singers on your charts. Bring in recordings of your favorite American singers. Compare them with other vocalists you have heard. Do you find characteristics that are similar? different? Do their reasons to sing seem the same or different?

The Gospel Tradition

OH HAPPY DAY

Words and Music by Edwin Hawkins

The gospel music of America is a sound heard in the Black communities throughout our country. Spirited, full, rich, and driven by powerful rhythms, gospel is an important part of America's folk sound.

Listen to "Oh Happy Day" and mark down the vocal characteristics you hear on your chart.

Copyright © 1969 Kama Rippa Music, Inc. and Edwin R. Hawkins Music Company
All rights administered by United Artists Music Co., Inc. Used by permission.

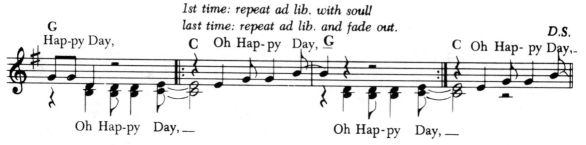

Plan your own gospel arrangement of "Oh Happy Day."
Perform in gospel style.
What vocal characteristics will you emphasize?

Improvise in a manner similar to the recording. Use these patterns for an introduction and on the ad-lib section.

Add hand clapping. Start with these patterns. Improvise others.

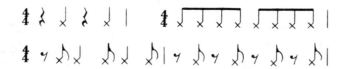

Embellish the vocal line.

Instrumental Sounds

Instruments, like voices, have distinctive characteristics that enable a performer to express a variety of ideas, feelings, and emotions.

As you see on the chart, the first five characteristics are the same for voices as well as instruments. An additional characteristic that contributes to the distinctive sound of an instrument is its **ENVELOPE:** the way the sound begins **(attack)**, continues, and ends **(decay).** ⟍___ or ⟍___

Listen to the sound of a single instrument. Use the chart to describe it.

CHART 11: Six Instrumental Characteristics

Title ....

Country ....

INSTRUMENT	SOUND STARTER
____ idiophone ____ aerophone	____ pluck ____ scrape
____ membranophone ____ electrophone	____ bow ____ blow
____ chordophone	____ hit ____ other

Quality   thin _____ rich
          1   2   3   4   5

Performance   choppy _____ flowing
Style
          1   2   3   4   5

Expression   limited _____ widely varied
          1   2   3   4   5

Register   very high _____ very low
          1   2   3   4   5

Tremolo   little _____ much
          1   2   3   4   5

Envelope:
  attack   sudden _____ gradual

  and
          1   2   3   4   5

  decay   sudden _____ gradual
          1   2   3   4   5

Idiophones

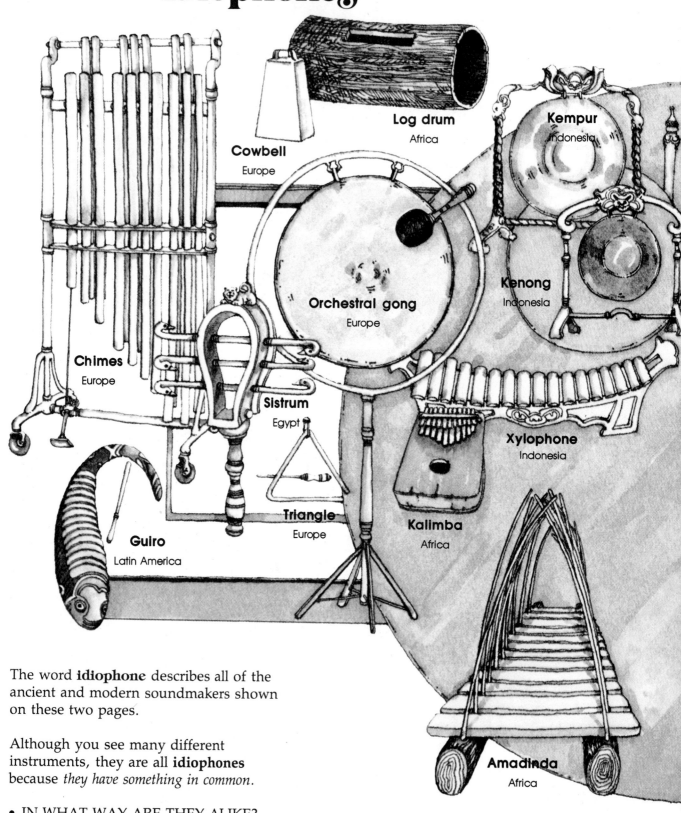

Log drum
Africa

Cowbell
Europe

Kempur
Indonesia

Chimes
Europe

Sistrum
Egypt

Orchestral gong
Europe

Kenong
Indonesia

Xylophone
Indonesia

Guiro
Latin America

Triangle
Europe

Kalimba
Africa

Amadinda
Africa

The word **idiophone** describes all of the ancient and modern soundmakers shown on these two pages.

Although you see many different instruments, they are all **idiophones** because *they have something in common.*

• IN WHAT WAY ARE THEY ALIKE?

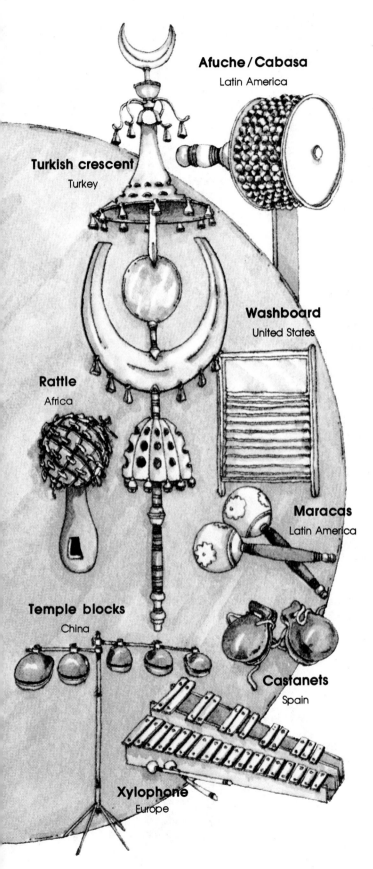

Afuche / Cabasa
Latin America

Turkish crescent
Turkey

Washboard
United States

Rattle
Africa

Maracas
Latin America

Temple blocks
China

Castanets
Spain

Xylophone
Europe

Listen to sounds of idiophones. Can you locate the picture of the soundmaker that produces each sound?

- ## SEMATIMBA NE KIKWABANGA

  Uganda

- ## HUDAN MAS (GOLDEN RAIN)

  Java

- ## TROUBLE IN MIND

  (excerpt)   United States

- ## LULLABY

  Central African Republic

Membranophones

Conga drum
Latin America

Snare drum
Europe

Tabla drums
India

Timpani
Europe

Taiko drum
Japan

Tambourine
Europe

Bongos
Latin America

The word **membranophone** describes all of the ancient and modern soundmakers on these two pages.

Although you may see many different instruments, they are all **membranophones** because *they have something in common.*

• IN WHAT WAY ARE THEY ALIKE?

Sogo drum
Africa

Kaganu drum
Africa

Kidi drum
Africa

Bass drum
Europe

Tenor drum
Europe

Tom tom
North America

Snare drum
Europe

Listen to sounds of membranophones.
Can you locate the picture of the
soundmaker that produces each sound?

• ATSIA

Ghana

• OLDEST RABBIT SONG

Sioux Indian

• SAETA

(excerpt)   Spain

Make Your Own Idiophones and Membranophones

Make your own idiophones and membranophones. Search for objects that would make good idiophones. What materials could you find to use as the vibrating membrane for a membranophone? What might you use for beaters or scrapers?

Collect your instruments.
Try out the sound quality of each.
Use these and other instruments to perform music of Africa and Java.

Music for Membranophones and Idiophones

To play this African Ewe Dance, you need:

- Three drums of varying pitch:
  Sogo—lowest
  Kaganu—middle
  Kidi—highest

- Sticks to strike the drums,
- *Axhatsi*—a gourd rattle, and
- *Gankogui*—a double bell.

ATSIA

(Excerpt)

Transcribed by James Koetting

African Ewe Dance Music

Gankogui	H		H		H	H		H		H		H
Sogo	o		o	♪	♪	♪	o		o	♪	♪	♪
Kaganu		o	o		o	o		o	o		o	o
Kidi	o			o		o			o		
Axhatsi	D			D			D			D		

o = Stick strikes drumhead and rebounds.   D = Strike rattle downward against your thigh.

♪ = Stick strikes drumhead and remains.   H = Play a high tone on gankogui.

HUDAN MAS

Transcribed by Jill Poris (Excerpt) Javanese Gamelan Music

Listen again to "Hudan Mas" (page 83). Then develop your own Javanese gamalan. What instruments can you find or make to suggest the sound of the instruments you hear?

On the right is a simplified score of the first melody in "Hudan Mas." To play it, you will need:

- *Sarons*—metal-keyed xylophones in several sizes. The smallest is the *Penong*. Find instruments that can play E♭, F, A, B♭, and C.

- Three Drums—low, middle, and high.

- Gongs (four kinds):
  - *Kempul*—suspended gongs. You need two with the pitches F and A.
  - *Kenong*—pitched gongs set in racks. You need E♭ and F.
  - *Ketuk*—small gong with a deadened sound.
  - *Gong*—largest, nonpitched gong with a deep sound.

The pitches in the score are written with numbers. You can approximate the gamelan tuning with these pitches:

2 = E♭ **3** = F   **5** = A   **6** = B♭   **7** = C

BEAT	Sarons	Penong	Ketuk	Kenong	Kempul	Gong	Drum
1	6	6 / 5	X				M
2	5	5 / 5					M
3	3	3 / 3	X				M
4	2	2 / 2		2			H
5	6	6 / 6	X				M
6	5	5 / 5			5		M
7	3	3 / 3	X				M
8	2	2 / 2		2			H
9	3	3 / 3	X				M
10	3	3 / 3			3		M
11	2	2 / 2	X				M
12	3	3 / 3		3			M / H
13	6	6 / -6	X				H / M
14	5	5 / 5			5		L / M
15	3	3 / 3	X				M / L
16	2	2 / 2		2		X	L

87

Chordophones

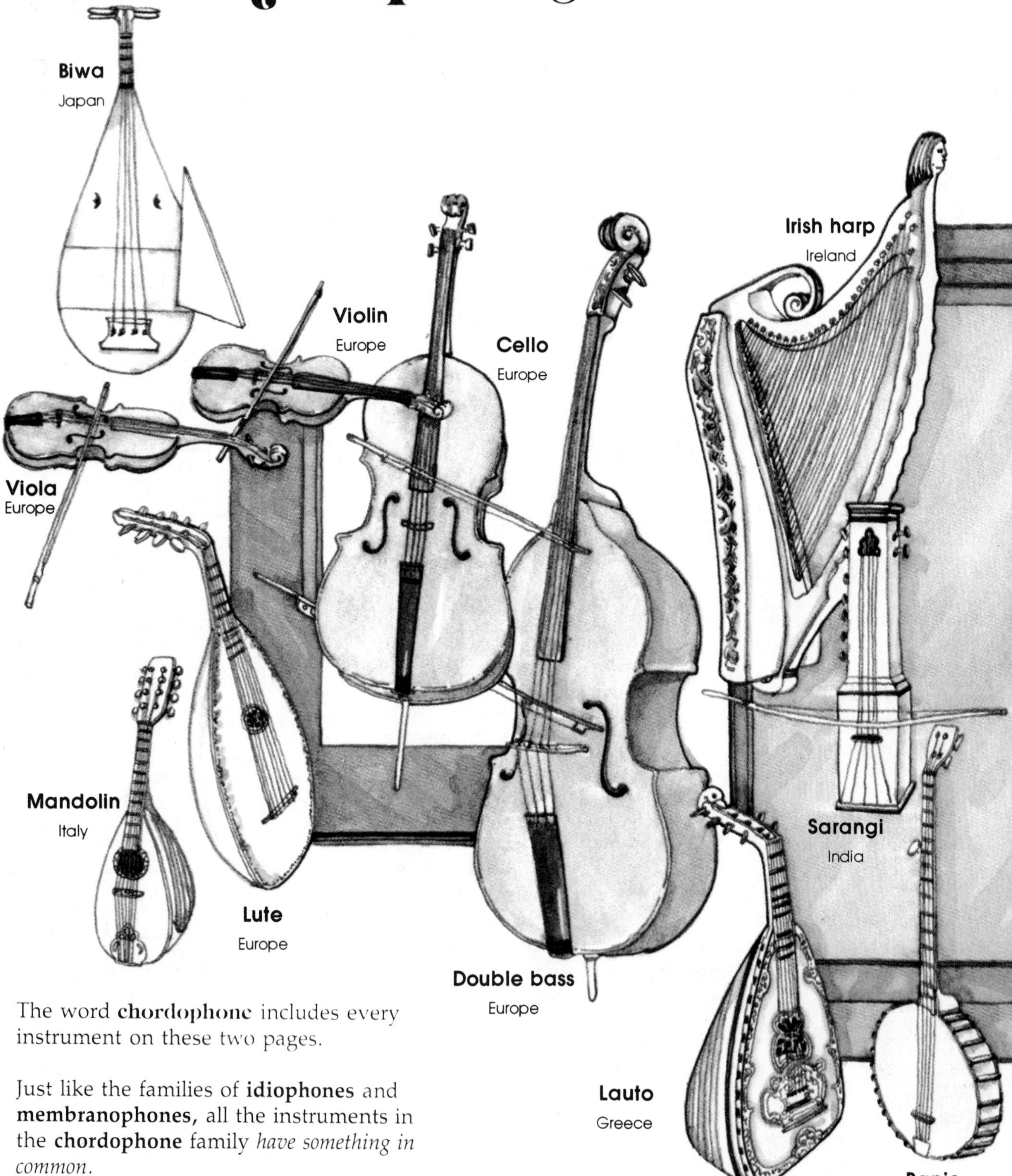

Biwa
Japan

Violin
Europe

Cello
Europe

Irish harp
Ireland

Viola
Europe

Mandolin
Italy

Lute
Europe

Double bass
Europe

Sarangi
India

Lauto
Greece

Banjo
United States

The word **chordophone** includes every instrument on these two pages.

Just like the families of **idiophones** and **membranophones,** all the instruments in the **chordophone** family *have something in common.*

• IN WHAT WAY ARE THEY ALIKE?

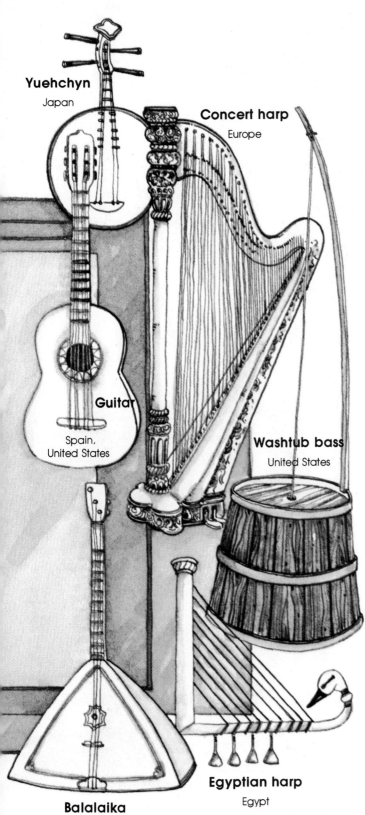

Yuehchyn
Japan

Concert harp
Europe

Guitar
Spain,
United States

Washtub bass
United States

Balalaika
Russia

Egyptian harp
Egypt

Listen to these examples of chordophones.
Can you locate the picture of the soundmaker that produces each sound?

• OGI NO MATO

(excerpt)   Japan

• WHAT MAKES MY
  BABY CRY

United States

• RAGHUVARĀNANNU

(excerpt)   South India

• COLOR HIM FOLKY

United States

KALAMATIANOS

(excerpt)   Greek Folk Dance

Instrumental music has been used to accompany the dances of people in many parts of the world throughout the ages. Learn to perform a traditional Greek chain dance. Dance it to the recording of "Kalamatianos."

Each measure has seven beats grouped 3 + 2 + 2. You must change the direction of your body at the beginning of *each* measure!

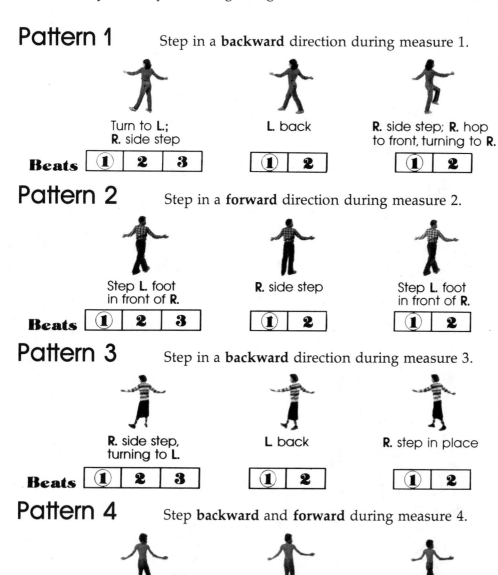

Pattern 1   Step in a **backward** direction during measure 1.

Turn to **L.**;
R. side step

L. back

R. side step; **R.** hop
to front, turning to **R.**

Beats | ① | 2 | 3 | | ① | 2 | | ① | 2 |

Pattern 2   Step in a **forward** direction during measure 2.

Step **L.** foot
in front of **R.**

R. side step

Step **L.** foot
in front of **R.**

Beats | ① | 2 | 3 | | ① | 2 | | ① | 2 |

Pattern 3   Step in a **backward** direction during measure 3.

R. side step,
turning to **L.**

L back

R. step in place

Beats | ① | 2 | 3 | | ① | 2 | | ① | 2 |

Pattern 4   Step **backward** and **forward** during measure 4.

Turn to **R.**
L. back

Step back with **R.**
to join **L**

Step **L.** foot
in front of **R.**

Beats | ① | 2 | 3 | | ① | 2 | | ① | 2 |

- Quickly return to the backward direction and repeat both patterns.
  - Continue the dance by repeating the same two-measure sequence.
    - The chain of dancers moves freely around the room following the leader.

The Hustle

HI! HI! HI!

by Tony Valie and Steve Martin

Learn to perform this American dance. Begin by forming rows that face forward. Upon each repetition of the complete dance, the rows turn a quarter circle to the left, back, right, and return to the original position **(B4).**

Follow the instructions as you listen to the music. The music and the dance steps move in groups of four.

Beat:	1	2	3	4
A	Tap **R** heel to front.	Repeat.	Bring **R** toe to **L** foot and tap.	Repeat.
B	Tap **R** heel to front.	Bring **R** toe to **L** foot and tap.	Point **R** toe out to **R** side.	Hop on **L** foot and kick off with **R** knee, turning ¼ circle.
C	**R** foot steps backward.	**L** foot steps backward.	**R** foot steps backward.	Flex **R** knee. (**R** foot still on ground.)
D	**L** foot steps forward.	**R** foot steps forward.	**L** foot steps forward.	Flex **L** knee.
E	**R** foot steps to **R** side.	Step together with **L** foot.	**R** foot steps to **R** side.	Flex **R** knee.
F	**L** foot steps to **L** side.	Step together with **R** foot.	**L** foot steps to **L** side.	Flex **L** knee.
G	Jump forward with both feet.	Flex both knees.	Jump backward with both feet.	Flex both knees.
H	Jump forward with both feet.	Jump backward with both feet.	Click heels.	Click heels.

Aerophones

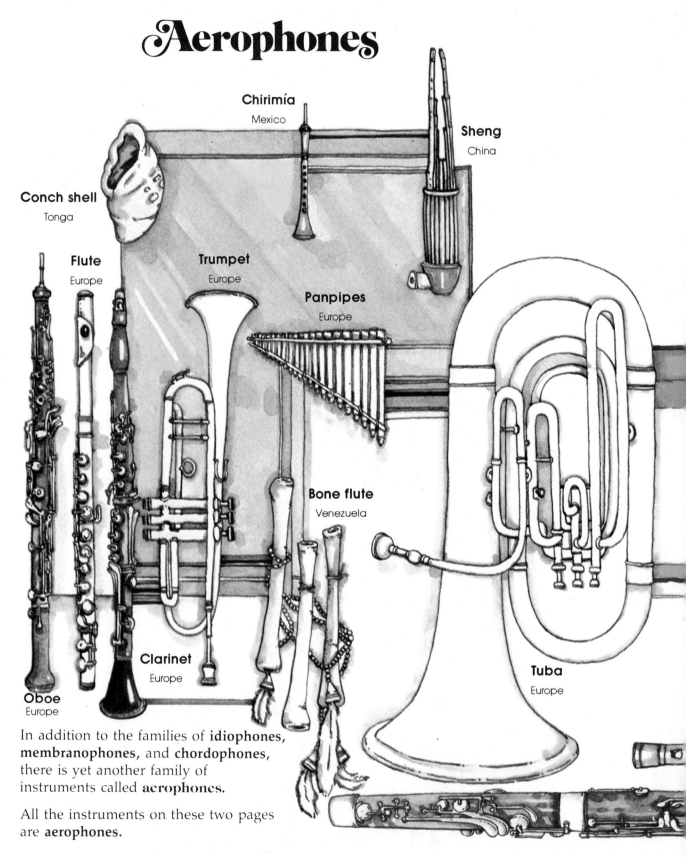

Chirimía
Mexico

Sheng
China

Conch shell
Tonga

Flute
Europe

Trumpet
Europe

Panpipes
Europe

Bone flute
Venezuela

Oboe
Europe

Clarinet
Europe

Tuba
Europe

In addition to the families of **idiophones**, **membranophones**, and **chordophones**, there is yet another family of instruments called **aerophones**.

All the instruments on these two pages are **aerophones**.

• IN WHAT WAY ARE THEY ALIKE?

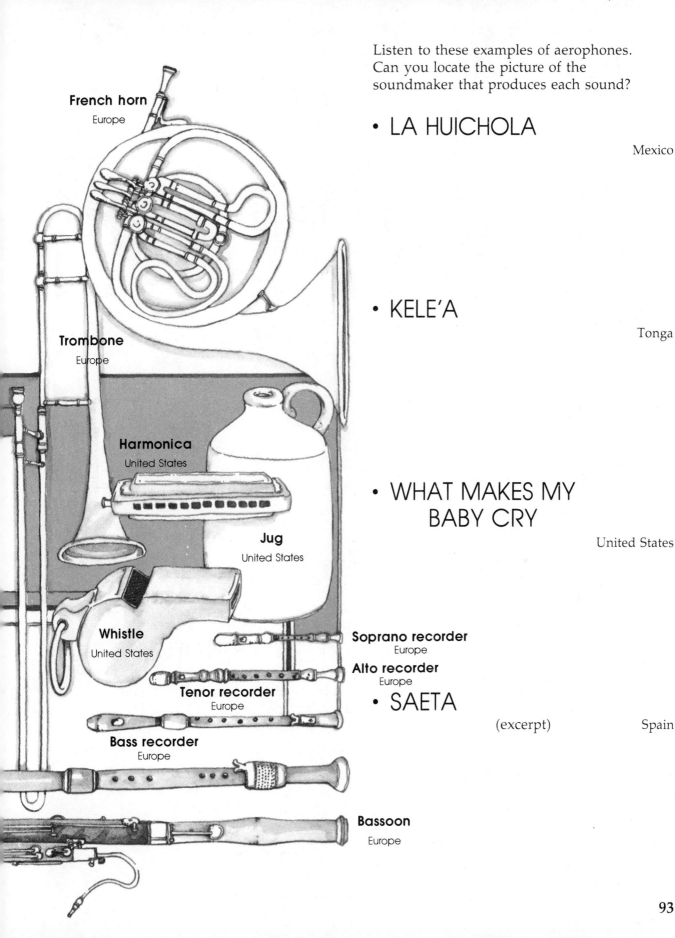

Listen to these examples of aerophones. Can you locate the picture of the soundmaker that produces each sound?

- LA HUICHOLA

  Mexico

- KELE'A

  Tonga

- WHAT MAKES MY BABY CRY

  United States

- SAETA

  (excerpt)   Spain

French horn
Europe

Trombone
Europe

Harmonica
United States

Jug
United States

Whistle
United States

Soprano recorder
Europe

Alto recorder
Europe

Tenor recorder
Europe

Bass recorder
Europe

Bassoon
Europe

An Aerophone Ensemble

From the time people first began inventing musical instruments, they have used materials from their environment. What objects can you find in your environment to use as an aerophone?

- Collect objects of several different sizes. Experiment with them to find good sounds and different pitches. What can you do to your aerophone to alter its pitch?
- Form small groups. Each group is to plan and perform a composition.
- Each member should make up a short, rhythmic pattern. Each pattern should be different. Devise a way to notate your pattern.
- Perform together by playing the patterns on your aerophones. Listen to each other's parts! Play your pattern when you feel it will sound right with the others. Remember to include some silence!

Try "Hocketing"

Form an ensemble of five aerophone players. Tune your instruments as closely as possible to steps 1, 2, 3, and 5 of a **major** scale.

Play this tune by "hocketing": each performer is to play just one of the pitches in the tune. You must think the rhythm of the piece as it is played, entering with your pitch at exactly the right time. If you play correctly, you will recognize a famous tune.

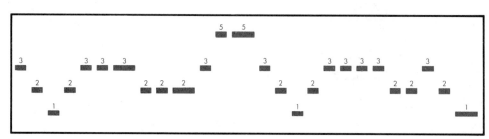

Electrophones ...the newest family

Electrophones—electronic instruments and conventional instruments that can modify their sound through electronics—have changed the great sound of our music. By these new means, our ears have been stretched to new capacities and our means of musical communication has indeed caused . . . a new journey through time and space!

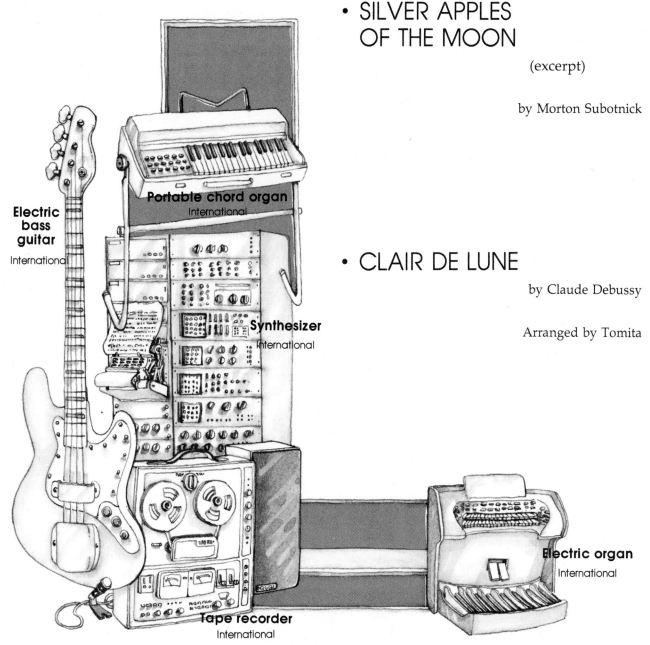

Electric bass guitar
International

Portable chord organ
International

Synthesizer
International

Tape recorder
International

Electric organ
International

- ## SILVER APPLES OF THE MOON

(excerpt)

by Morton Subotnick

- ## CLAIR DE LUNE

by Claude Debussy

Arranged by Tomita

What Do You Hear?

You have been learning to identify and categorize sounds of the world's instruments according to individual sounds within "families." Can you now use that information to identify and describe instruments when many sound colors are mixed?

Listen to some examples. You will need to listen several times. Each time focus on a different sound characteristic. Begin by trying to identify the family to which the sounds belong and the manner in which the sound is started.

You may need to mark more than one place along the scale of a particular sound characteristic to describe what you hear at any one time. If the mix changes within that category, mark the next segment along the scale.

CHART 12: Sounds of Mixed Groups

Title . . . .   Country . . . .
Voices . . . .

INSTRUMENTS:
_____ Idiophones
_____ Membranophones
_____ Chordophones
_____ Aerophones

SOUNDS STARTED:
_____ plucked   _____ scraped
_____ bowed   _____ blown
_____ hit   _____ other
_____ shaken

| Quality | thin / rich | 1 | 2 | 3 | 4 | 5 |

| Performance Style | choppy / flowing | 1 | 2 | 3 | 4 | 5 |

| Expression | limited / widely varied | 1 | 2 | 3 | 4 | 5 |

| Register | high / low | 1 | 2 | 3 | 4 | 5 |

| Tremolo | much / little | 1 | 2 | 3 | 4 | 5 |

96

You Make the Mix

- Perform the following canon.
- Use two to eight instruments.
- The instruments enter one measure apart.

The way in which you mix the instruments will affect the final sound of your ensemble. Experiment with different combinations.

- instruments from the same family
- instruments from different families
- instruments having the same range
- instruments having different ranges
- instruments that sound in different keys
- instruments that are pitched with instruments that are nonpitched
- nonpitched instruments

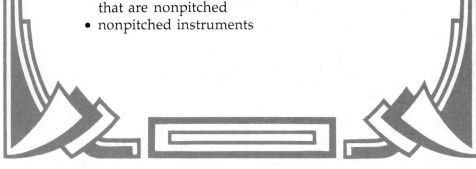

Experiment: Use the above mixing ideas as well as your own alone or in combination with each other! In how many traditional or nontraditional ways can you mix the sounds of instruments?

Mixing Colors

CLAIR DE LUNE

from *Suite Bergamasque*

by Claude Debussy

Listen to the same piece of music performed by three different "mixes."

Small Ensemble   **Synthesizer**   **Large Ensemble**

Describe what you hear on your chart of "Sounds of Mixed Groups."
Compare the three charts. How did the different mixes affect the music?
Do you have a preference? What influenced your choice?

Rhythms of the Whole Earth

Music begins with a single sound. As other sounds follow and flow through time, we become aware of rhythm.

Compare ways that sounds may be combined to create musical rhythm.
Try to turn each illustration of rhythm into sound.

BEAT

Most of the world's music moves in relation to an underlying beat or pulse that may be regular

● ● ● ● ● ● ●

or irregular.

● ● ● ●●●● ● ● ● ● ● ● ● ●

ACCENTS

Sometimes these beats are grouped through the use of accents that may result in regular groupings

● ● ● ● ● ● ●
>   >

or in groupings that are irregular.

● ● ● ● ● ● ● ●
>   >   > >

The beat and accent may be strongly sounded or almost absent.

RHYTHMIC FLOW

A single rhythmic line may move with an irregular flow

▬ ▬ ▬ ▬ ▬ ▬ ▬ ▬ ▬ ▬ ▬ ▬ ● ● ▬ ▬ ▬ ● ● ● ● ● ● ● ● ▬ ▬

or with a more regular flow that is controlled by an underlying beat (even though the beat is not sounded).

▬ ▬ ▬ ▬ ▬ ▬ ▬ ▬ ▬ ▬ ▬ ▬ ▬

WORKING TOGETHER

Two or more rhythmic lines may be sounded simultaneously. They might:
- move with an irregular flow and be unrelated to each other,

- move with a regular pattern and be closely related to each other,

- or one line might move irregularly against one or more regular patterns.

Listen to Musical Rhythm

Listen again to music of the world's people. On a chart of "Rhythm" mark an X along each line that best describes what you hear.

CHART 13: Rhythm

Title _____ Country _____

Beat Feeling

weak   strong
1   2   3   4   5

irregular   regular
1   2   3   4   5

Accent

unaccented   accented
1   2   3   4   5

Flow

irregular   regular
1   2   3   4   5

Working Together

unrelated   related
1   2   3   4   5

Melody Moves in Shapes and Curves...

The music of the world moves rhythmically through time. It also moves through "space," creating a shape called **melody.** Just as each culture organizes rhythm in distinctive ways, each group of people may emphasize certain melodic shapes. Experiment with these examples.

• Shape 1

Start very low on a steady "ah." Quickly swoop up high, then go back down to your original low pitch. Can you sing the same shape at a very slow tempo without going so high?

• Shape 2

Make an "oo" sound and perform this shape at different tempos. Can you keep the same shape but widen your singing range?

• Shape 3

On the sound "ee," start high and slowly slide to a very low "oo." Then make a little swoop upward. Try other performances with different tempos within a more limited range.

• Shape 4

Perform this sound-and-silence shape at any speed and with any vowel sound. Pay attention to the **comparative** lengths of sounds and silences.

• Shape 5 ?

On a separate piece of paper, draw a melodic shape of your own design. Then perform it for your classmates. Have them draw what they hear. Compare their versions with yours. How accurate was your performance? How accurately did your classmates listen?

...from Highs to Lows to Highs and Lows

Listen to Melody

Complete a chart of "Melody" for each melodic example you hear.

In the long box next to **SHAPE**, draw the approximate shape of each melody. Is it

undulating 〰〰〰　　　　**arched** ⌒

terraced 〜〜　　　　**irregular** 〰

or a combination of these?

Next mark an X somewhere along the **RANGE** line.
Is the melody moving in

a **narrow range** 〰　　　　a **wide range** 〰

or somewhere in between?

Then mark an X somewhere along the **MOTION** line.
Is the melody moving by

steps ▪▪▪　　　　**skips** ▪▪▪

or in a combination of both?

CHART 14: Melody

Title _____　　　　Country _____

- Shape

- Range　　　very narrow　　　　　　　　　　　　very wide
　　　　　　　/_____/_____/_____/_____/

- Motion　　　mostly steps　　　　　　　　　　　mostly skips
　　　　　　　/_____/_____/_____/_____/

103

form

Here is the way the first musicians might have started to make music.

They might have begun with a single small idea or **motive,**

Ba - nu - wa, ba - nu - wa, ba - nu - wa yo.___

which perhaps was repeated,

Ba - nu - wa, ba - nu - wa, ba - nu - wa yo.___

perhaps with a small change,

Ba - nu - wa, ba - nu - wa, ba - nu - wa yo.___

or **variation.**

Ba - nu - wa, ba - nu - wa, ba - nu - wa yo.___

Then a new idea might have been introduced for **contrast,**

A - la - no, neh - ni - o la - no, A -

the original idea returned,

Ba - nu - wa, ba - nu - wa, ba - nu - wa yo.___

or other new ideas might have been introduced and combined.

Create Your Own Form

Use ideas on page 104 and at the top of this page.

- Some voices begin with the first **motive.**
- Continue while others add **variations.**
- A few singers might introduce **contrast** while the original motive is continued.
- Repeat the motive many times. Change dynamics. End very softly.
- Begin the new musical idea in the same way. Some may sing the motive, then add other voices. How will you end?

Listening for Form

Listen to music from different parts of the world. Complete your chart of "Musical Form" to describe what you notice about the form of each example.

CHART 15: Musical Form

Title ....

Repetition	seldom occurs				often occurs
	1	2	3	4	5

Variation	seldom occurs				often occurs
	1	2	3	4	5

Contrast	seldom occurs				often occurs
	1	2	3	4	5

Texture

Texture is the way musical lines are put together:
- one line or many lines at the same time;
- lines moving together or independently;
- musical lines that are close together or far apart.

Create Different Textures

MONOPHONY   A single musical line.

Good   news,   Char - i - ot's a - com - in', Good   news,

Char - i - ot's a - com - in', Good news,   Char - i - ot's a - com - in' and I

don't want   it   to   leave   a - me   be - hind.

DRONE   One or two pitches continuously sounded as the only accompaniment to the melody.

Some may play or sing this drone while others sing "Good News."

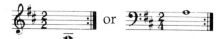

UNISON AND CHORDS Performers sing or play the same line but sometimes divide into different pitches.

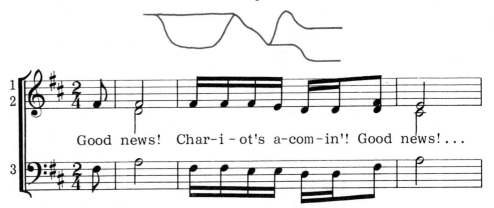

Good news! Char-i-ot's a-com-in'! Good news!...

PARALLEL MOTION The same or similar melody is performed simultaneously at different pitch levels.

Can you continue this parallel motion along with the melody?

Good news! Char - i - ot's a-com - in'!...

HOMOPHONY A main melody is backed up by supporting lines of harmonies.

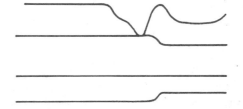

Some sing the melody while others sing this part.

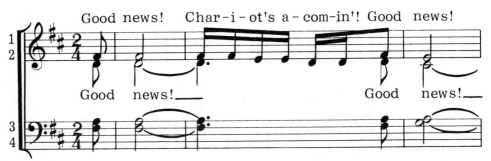

Good news! Char-i-ot's a-com-in'! Good news!

Good news!___ Good news!___

POLYPHONY   Each part has its own melody and rhythm.

Some sing the chorus of "Good News." Others sing the verse at the same time.

Verse

There'll be peace and free-dom in this world, I know;

Peace and free-dom in this world, I know; Peace and free-dom in this

world. I know, and I don't want it to leave a - me be - hind.

TEXTURAL DENSITY   The thinness or thickness of the texture.

thin   thick

Experiment with thin texture. Sing or play two or three lines as far apart in range as possible. Now try a thick texture. Divide into five or six small groups. Each group performs a different part. Combine several of the types of texture given such as polyphony, homophony, and drone.

Listen to music of different people. For each example, mark the terms on your chart of "Musical Texture" that describe the texture you hear.

monophony   **parallel motion**
drone   **homophony**
unison and chords **polyphony**

Was the texture thick? thin?

FANTASIA IN C FOR PIANO, CHORUS, AND ORCHESTRA, OP. 80

Excerpt

by Ludwig van Beethoven

1

Interplay of piano and orchestra. Imitation as high voices enter and low voices echo.

SCHMEICHELND HOLD

2

Homophonic texture like a chorale or hymn. Timbre: high voices accompanied by solo piano.

SCHMEICHELND HOLD UND LEIBLICH

3

Homophonic texture: Men's voices accompanied by piano and *pizzicato* strings.

WENN DER TÖNE ZAUBER WALTEN

4

Homophonic texture, now thicker: full chorus, orchestra, and piano.

GROSSES, DAS IN'S HERZ

5

Piano alternates with voices and orchestra.

NEHMT HIN, NEHMT HIN

6

NEHMT DENN HIN, IHR SCHÖNEN

Polyphonic texture.
Low voices begin,
high voices imitate. As
theme is extended, texture
changes, becoming more
homophonic.

7

NEHMT DENN HIN, IRH SCHÖNEN SEELEN

**Homophonic vocal
texture, piano and orchestra.**

8

NEHMT DENN HIN, IHR SCHÖNEN

**Return of polyphonic
texture,** becoming
homophonic.

9

NEHMT DENN HIN, IRH SCHÖNEN SEELEN

**Homophonic vocal
texture.**

10

**Interplay between
piano and orchestra.**

The Music of Today Is the Music of People in All Our Yesterdays

There is no completely "new" music. What we call "new"
grows   out   of
our ability to use and reuse the same ideas
in different shapes,
in different forms,
and with ever-changing sound resources.

MONKEY CHANT

Arranged by Jon Field
and Tony Duhig

Traditional

KALAGALA EBWEMBE

(excerpt)
from *Africanus
Brasileiras Americanus*

Arranged by Paul Winter

Traditional Ugandan Song

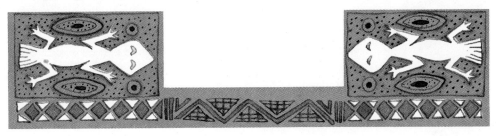

Music and Your Career

Your interest and skill in music can be used as a hobby for your own enjoyment or in work that will become your professional career. Many professions and businesses you may not have thought about are open to a person who develops a solid background in music. On the opposite page is a chart with information about careers you might think about if you like music. Study the chart, select the careers that interest you, and find out more about them. Interview people who have musical jobs such as the music faculty in your school. You might ask some of the following questions.

- How old were you when you first became interested in music? What were the circumstances?

    - Did you play an instrument? Did you take private lessons or did you study in school?

        - Did you concentrate on one style of music or did you explore a wide variety of musical styles?

- At what point did you know you wanted a career in music? How did you go about pursuing your career? Did you need any additional skills or training for this profession?

    - Who were the people who influenced your decisions? your career?

        - What advice would you give to a young person considering a career in music?

Share your interviews in class.

Career	Employment Opportunities	Personal Qualifications	Skills and Educational Requirements
COMPOSER	• writing for publication • college teacher • popular music, television films, advertising	• unusual musical talent • creative ability • unusual motivation	• study with composers • knowledge of capabilities of voice and instruments • knowledge of music theory and musical styles
CONDUCTOR	• orchestra, band, opera, dance band, chorus • college or high school teacher	• unusual musical talent • ability to direct people • dynamic and attractive personality	• excellent basic musical training • training in conducting • knowledge of music literature
PROFESSIONAL PERFORMER	• concert soloist • orchestra, band • rock or jazz group • radio, television	• musical talent • physical stamina • motivation to continue to study and improve • pleasing stage personality	• excellent basic musicianship • superior performance skills • knowledge of repertoire
CHURCH MUSICIAN	• performer or choir director in church or synagogue	• musical talent • ability to work with others	• basic musicianship • familiarity with liturgies • knowledge of scared repertoire
TEACHER	• public or private school • college • private studio	• musical talent • enjoy working with people	• basic musicianship • college and/or graduate degree • continuous study
MUSIC LIBRARIAN	• college • public library • orchestra, band, radio, television stations	• enjoy books and records • knowledge of music literature • ability to keep accurate records	• degree in library science • degree in music
MUSIC JOURNALIST OR CRITIC	• freelance • staff of magazine or newspaper	• aptitude for writing • ability to work under pressure	• knowledge of music • training in journalism and musical performance
MUSIC THERAPIST	• hospitals • clinics • corrective institutions	• musical talent • understanding of handicapped people • desire to help people	• degree in music with training in therapy • facility at piano or guitar • knowledge of physiology and psychology
STAGE MANAGER	• opera houses, theaters, repertory companies, companies for musical productions	• ability to work under pressure • ability to work with others • ability to organize	• knowledge of music • knowledge of technical aspects of theater
ARTIST AND CONCERT MANAGER	• private business • orchestras and other touring groups	• administrative ability • ability with figures and dates • ability to work with people	• background in music • knowledge of business practices
RECORD PRODUCER	• record companies • private business	• work well under pressure • persistent and meticulous worker • diplomatic	• knowledge of music; ability to read score • knowledge of recording equipment
MUSICAL SCHOLAR (MUSICOLOGIST OR ETHNOMUSICOLOGIST)	• college teacher • writer for specialized publications	• aptitude for scholarly research • interest in a wide variety of music	• extensive knowledge of music literature and theory • research and writing skills • knowledge of foreign languages • writing and speaking ability
TUNER-TECHNICIAN	• private business • manufacturing	• mechanical ability • interest in music, musical instruments	• work experience in tuning, repairing, and manufacturing

Unit III
PLAYING FOLK INSTRUMENTS

Skiffling Around

CHART 17: Commitment to Musical Learning (4)

In this section you will have the opportunity to:

Rhythm Instruments

— maintain a steady beat
— perform a repetitive pattern
— improvise interesting rhythms
— learn a rhythm from notation
— alter the quality of
   sound on your instrument

Melody Instruments

— play in tune
— play with rhythmic accuracy
— learn a melody by ear
— learn a melody from notation
— play with a pleasing tone
   quality

Harmony Instruments

— play chords in tune
— improvise an accompaniment
— tune your instrument

— perform with rhythmic and
   tonal accuracy
— read chord charts
— play with a pleasing tone
   quality

- Which of these can you now do independently?
- In which of these areas will you commit yourself to becoming more independent?

Skiffling Around

"Skiffling" is informal music-making using homemade and store-bought instruments. In a typical skiffle band, the instruments are grouped something like this:

Melody

Rhythm

Melody and Harmony

Bass

Melody and Drone

- Listen to a skiffle band.
- Can you identify the instruments that take solo "rides"?

BILE THEM CABBAGE DOWN

MAMA DON'T 'LOW

Homemade instruments used in skiffling have their roots in the musical traditions of the British Isles and Africa. The **spoons** and the **limberjack** are often used to accompany British or American fiddle tunes and folk songs. The **washboard, washtub bass, jug,** and **kazoo** have long been popular in Afro-American blues bands and jug bands. Even today, any of these homemade instruments might be heard in American old-timey, country, bluegrass, blues, or jug bands.

WHAT MAKES MY BABY CRY?

THE SPOONS

Some American folk instruments are *found* at home rather than *made* at home. The spoons are one example of "found sounds." They are a must for skiffling, adding lively rhythmic accompaniments.

Listen to the spoons.

SOLDIER'S JOY

Hold the Spoons

Hold the Bottom Spoon
- Place one spoon between the index and middle fingers of the hand you write with.
- Keep the round side *up*.

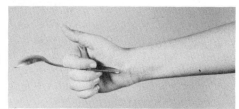

Add the Top Spoon
- Place the second spoon over the index finger.
- Keep the round side *down*.
- Keep the top spoon parallel to the bottom spoon.
- Be sure the spoon ends are wedged into your palm.

The *thumb* should be lying on the top spoon. The index finger keeps the spoons apart. The other three fingers hold the spoons in place.

Play the Spoons

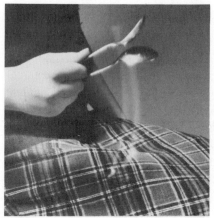

Sit down. Hold the spoons over your thigh. Tap your thigh lightly with the spoons, keeping a steady beat.

Start slowly; practice until you can play in a fast tempo without losing the steady beat—or your spoons!

Next, place your free hand about four inches above the spoons so that the spoons hit your hand just before they hit your thigh.

Try playing in this rhythm:
"THIGH-hand-THIGH, THIGH-hand-THIGH—
DUM-de-DUM, DUM-de-DUM, D-d-D, D-d-D, D-d-D"

To really impress your friends, you need to learn the "roll." Extend your top hand outward as if you were going to shake hands. Spread the fingers wide apart. Turn the palm slightly upward.

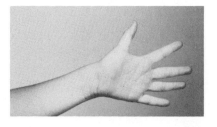

SPOONS

steady beat–divided beat–roll

Now, run the spoons across the fingers, top to bottom. Land on your thigh. The rhythm should sound like this:
"de-de-de-de-de-DUM, d-d-d-d-D, d-d-d-d-D"

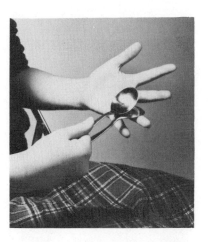

Try accompanying yourself as you sing a familiar folk tune such as "Skip to My Lou." When you have the techniques mastered, try playing along with

SOLDIER'S JOY

THE JUG

The **jug** is another "found sound" that is a very popular American skiffle instrument. It is easy to find, inexpensive to own, and handy to carry around! One reason it is so popular is its unique tonal quality.

Although we may think of the jug as a novelty or comical instrument, it originally served a serious purpose. It provided the bass accompaniment and melody lines that we associate today with the sound of the string bass.

WHAT MAKES MY BABY CRY?

Play the Jug

To get started, you must first find a jug made out of crockery or glass. A jug with a handle is easier to hold while you play. The size and shape will affect the tonal quality, so try several jugs until you find one you like.

"Buzz" your lips like a trumpet player. Hold the jug close enough to your lips to "catch" and resonate the sound.

You may have to experiment moving the jug around until you find just the right position to produce the sound.

118

To change pitch, tighten or relax your buzzing lips.

Listen to some jug playing.

SKIP TO MY LOU

WORRIED MAN BLUES

Try an oom-pah bass with one of the jug-band recordings you just heard.

Begin to Skiffle
- Find a spoon player and a few friends to sing. Get your jug and try some of these songs.
- Can you tell when to change the pitch of the jug?

Foot-Stompers	Easy-Goin' Folk Songs
SHE'LL BE COMIN' 'ROUND THE MOUNTAIN	**HOME ON THE RANGE**
SKIP TO MY LOU	**ON TOP OF OLD SMOKY**
OH, SUSANNA	**DOWN IN THE VALLEY**
THIS LAND IS YOUR LAND	**WORRIED MAN BLUES**

THE KAZOO

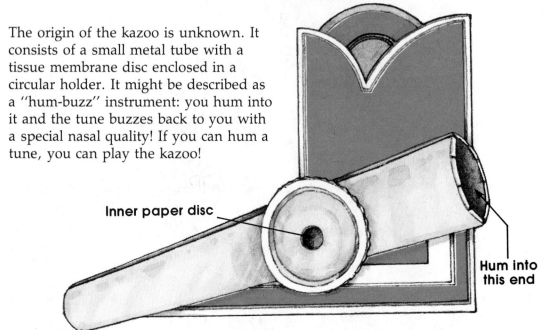

The origin of the kazoo is unknown. It consists of a small metal tube with a tissue membrane disc enclosed in a circular holder. It might be described as a "hum-buzz" instrument: you hum into it and the tune buzzes back to you with a special nasal quality! If you can hum a tune, you can play the kazoo!

Inner paper disc

Hum into this end

You can purchase a kazoo or make your own from a comb and a piece of very thin paper. Tissue paper, waxed paper, or onionskin are best.

You may want to experiment with different sizes and shapes of combs to discover what happens to the tone quality. Fold the paper in half and put the comb into the fold. Then cut around the paper to fit the shape of the comb.

Play the Kazoo

- Place the comb wrapped in paper against your lips.
- Hum. Did you get a "buzz" tone? Then you are ready to join the skiffle group!

THE WASHBOARD

Along with the spoons, one of the most popular "found" instruments is the **washboard.** It was first popular in the rural blues bands of the 1920's. You can still hear it in folk and country music bands today.

Washboards can be held in a variety of ways. Some performers hang the washboard around their necks with a strap so that they can play rhythms with both hands. Virgil Perkins, a rural blues musician, mounted his washboard on a stand. Listen to the variety of rhythms and tonal qualities he is able to produce.

TROUBLE IN MIND
(excerpt)

Play the Washboard

The hardest part of playing a washboard may be finding one! Hunt for an old washboard, or you may find new ones in some hardware stores. You will also need three thimbles.

- Put the thimbles on the thumb and first two fingers of your writing hand.
- Hold the washboard with the other hand, cradling it against you.
- Tap and scrape your thimbled fingers on the ridges of the board. You can even tap on the wooden frame. Hum, whistle, or sing an old tune, such as "Old Joe Clark," and accompany yourself.

Listen to a demonstration of some of the sounds and rhythms you can improvise on your washboard.

WASHBOARD

THE WASHTUB BASS

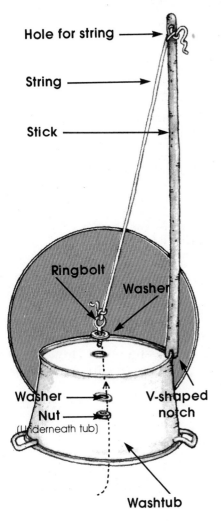

Hole for string

String

Stick

Ringbolt

Washer

Washer

Nut
(Underneath tub)

V-shaped notch

Washtub

You may decide to make a washtub bass for the same reason that this instrument became popular in the early 1900's—its cost! Although people could order musical instruments from a catalogue, a string bass cost well over $20.00! So people turned to materials at hand and created their own instruments. A well-constructed and well-played washtub bass sounds very much like a string bass.

Make a Washtub Bass

You Will Need
- A *tub* or pail large enough to make a deep, resonant sound, but small enough for you to carry.
- A *stick* at least 4' long. Use an old broomstick, mop handle, or a length of 1" doweling.
- A *string.* Use lightweight clothes line, nylon cord, or a real string-bass string.
- Some *hardware:* A 1" "ring" or "eye" bolt, two metal washers, and one nut.

Follow These Steps
1. Turn the washtub *upside down.* Drill a hole in the middle of the washtub that is equal to the diameter of the bolt (1").
2. Place one washer against the bottom of the tub and put the bolt through the hole in the washtub. Turn the washtub rightside up, keeping the bolt in position. Put the washer and nut on the end of the bolt. Then tighten the nut until the bolt is secure.
3. Drill a hole in the stick about 2" from the top.
4. Turn the tub upside down again. Make a V-shaped notch in the bottom of the stick so that it can fit over the rim of the tub.
5. Tie one end of the string to the bolt.
6. Pass the other end of the string through the hole in the top of the stick. Tie a knot so that the string is taut enough to hold the stick upright.

Play the Washtub Bass

To produce different bass notes on the washtub bass, you need to change the tension of the string. You can do this by pulling back on the stick with one hand as you pluck with the other to create a "walking bass" . . .

WASHTUB BASS

walking bass

or "fret" the string to make an "oom-pah bass" accompaniment.

WASHTUB BASS

root bass

Which method is the performer using in this performance?

DEEP FORK RIVER BLUES

There are many "tricks of the trade" that you will pick up as you practice. For example:
- Put your foot on the tub's edge to keep it from "dancing" away;
- Wear a glove on your "plucking" hand to prevent blisters and sore fingers;
- Prop up one side of the tub with a block of wood to allow more sound to escape.

BILE THEM CABBAGE DOWN

American Folk Song

Choose your instrument. Then join the recording of "Bile Them Cabbage Down." Can you add the root bass?

THE LIMBERJACK

If you have ever seen a **limberjack** in a store or museum, you may have thought it was a toy. Actually, it is an authentic rhythm instrument used in folk music-making, particularly in the mountains of the southern United States.

> The limberjack imitates a style of solo folk dancing called "step dancing" or "clog dancing." The dancer not only dances *to* the music, but also adds to its rhythm with the clicking sounds of his or her dancing feet!

Listen to a limberjack.

LIMBERJACK

OLD JOE CLARK

Make a Limberjack

You Will Need
- A 4″ × 6″ piece of ½″ thick *hard wood*.
- One 5″ length of ¼″ *doweling*.
- A 19″ length of coathanger or lighter *wire* or fish line.
- A 3½″ × 5″ piece of ¼″ plywood.
- A *yardstick*.

Prepare the Parts of the Limberjack
1. Make your pattern by copying the parts on page 125. Outline the patterns onto your piece of hard wood.
2. With a coping saw or jig saw, cut out the **body**. Drill ⅛″ holes at the shoulder- and hip-level of the body as shown by the dotted lines on the pattern. Drill a ¼″ hole in the center, as illustrated by the dotted circle, so that the ¼″ dowel fits snugly into the hole.
3. With a back saw, cut out eight **joints**, each 2″ × ½″ × ½″. Drill ⅛″ holes in both ends of four of the joints, and ⅛″ holes in only one end of the other four joints.
4. With a back saw, cut out **two feet**, each 1″ × ½″ × ½″.
5. Sand the rough edges off each piece before assembling the limberjack.

124

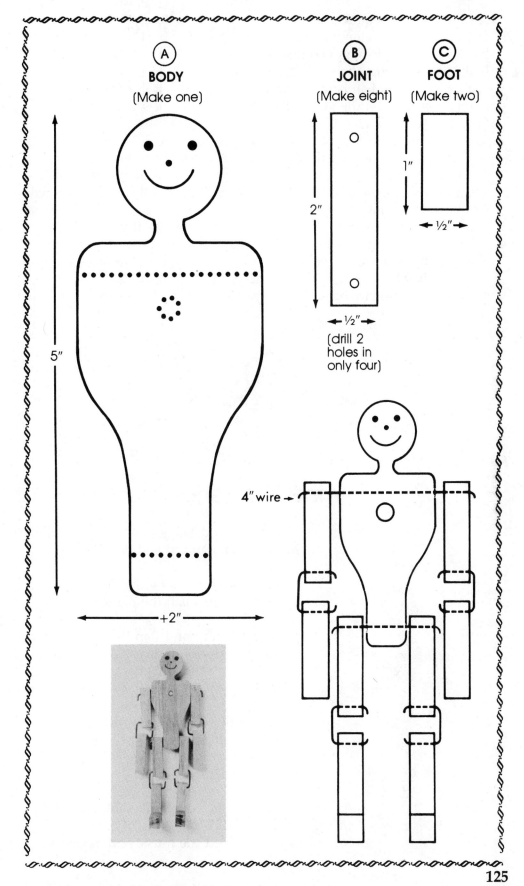

A
BODY
(Make one)

B
JOINT
(Make eight)

C
FOOT
(Make two)

5"

2"

1"

½"

½"

(drill 2
holes in
only four)

+2"

4" wire →

Assemble the Limberjack

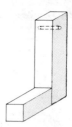

1. Using carpenter's glue, glue each foot block to a lower leg joint so that it looks like this from the side. Use C-clamps or rubber bands to hold the parts together until the glue dries (about half an hour).

2. Cut the wire or fish line into these approximate lengths: five 3" pieces and one 4" piece. Thread the wire through the body and joints, bending it into loops as shown in the picture on page 125, until the limberjack is completely assembled. Do not fasten the wire too tightly or the joints will not be able to move freely to "dance."

3. You may paint, varnish, or decorate your limberjack if you wish.

4. Insert the dowel into the hole in the back of the body until one end is flush with the front of the body. You can carry your limberjack more easily if the stick is removable, so do not glue it in place.

5. Glue the plywood to the end of the yardstick to form a platform for your dancer.

Play the Limberjack

Sit on the yardstick so that the platform reaches to about the end of your knees.

Hold the limberjack by the dowel so that its feet almost touch the platform.

With the other hand, tap the yardstick so that the platform bounces. You do not need to move the limberjack up and down.

That's all there is to it! As you tap faster or slower, the limberjack will produce different rhythms as its feet touch the bouncing platform.

With practice, you will be able to make the limberjack dance fascinating rhythms. Start the music and begin the dance!

OLD JOE CLARKE

American Folk Song

Verse

1. Old Joe Clarke he had a house,
2. Old Joe Clarke he had a mule,
3. Old Joe had a yel - low cat,
4. I went down to Old Joe's house,

Fif - teen stor - ies high, And ev - 'ry stor - y
It's name was Mor - gan Brown, And ev - 'ry tooth in
She'd nei - ther sing nor pray, Stuck her head in the
Nev - er been there be - fore, He slept on a

in that house Was filled with chick - en pie.
that mule's head Was six - teen in - ches 'round.
but - ter - milk jar To work her sins a - way.
feath - er bed And I slept on the floor.

Chorus

Fare ye well, Old Joe Clarke, Fare ye well, I say.

Fare ye well, Old Joe Clarke, I'm a - goin' a - way.

5. Sixteen horses in my team,
   The leaders they are blind,
   And every time the sun goes down
   There's a pretty girl on my mind.

   chorus

6. Eighteen miles of mountain road
   And fifteen miles of sand,
   If I ever travel this road again,
   I'll be a married man.

   chorus

THE MOUTHBOW

The mouthbow is a very ancient musical instrument. It is known in both Afro-American and Anglo-American folk music. Listen to the sound of the mouthbow in "Groundhog." Notice that there are two different sounds: the sound of the *tune* and the sound of the string's *drone*.

GROUNDHOG

Make a Mouthbow

You Will Need
- A yardstick.
- A violin or ukulele peg.
- A string such as a *nonwound* steel guitar string with loop or ball end.
- A large, flat guitar pick or homemade plastic pick.

Assemble the Mouthbow
1. Punch or drill a 1/16" hole about 1" from one end of the yardstick.
2. Drill a hole about 2" from the opposite end so that the peg will go about halfway in without forcing.
3. Insert the peg into the large hole.
4. Attach the string by putting it through the small hole at the top of the stick, then through the loop or ball end of the string, and finally through the hole in the peg.

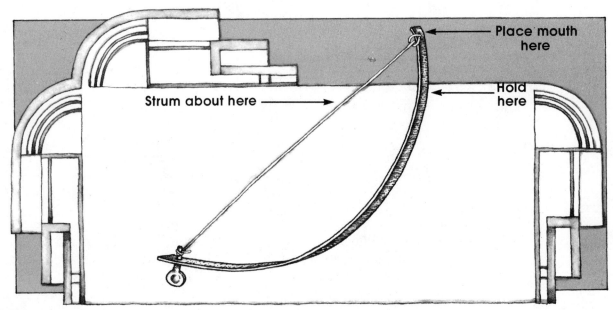

Strum about here →
Place mouth here
Hold here

Play the Mouthbow

1. Tighten the string as you bend the bow: Place the end with the small hole against the floor. Gently bend the wood with your hand as you tighten the string by turning the peg. The tightness of the string will determine the drone pitch of your mouthbow.
2. Hold the bow in your left hand, about 6″ from the end with the small hole. (Left handers, reverse instructions.)

3. Hold the flat side of the bow against your right cheek so that your lips, slightly opened, press against the bow near the upper end of the string.

   Your mouth is the resonating chamber that will amplify the sound of the bow as well as make the melody pitches.

4. With the pick in your other hand, pluck up and down the string as you open and close your mouth. Do you hear the pitch change? Keep experimenting until you can control the sound and the pitch.
5. Choose a lively song, such as "Skip to My Lou," and play the tune. Can you hear the string drone as well?

THE HARMONICA

The harmonica is a well-traveled instrument! Explorers have played the harmonica during expeditions to both poles, to the top of Mt. Everest, and even into outer space. Astronaut Walter Schirra played the harmonica while orbiting the earth in *Gemini VI!*

Harmonica-playing styles are as numerous as the performers who choose the harmonica as their favorite instrument. Listen to the expressive sound of the harmonica accompanying "The Colorado Trail."

THE COLORADO TRAIL

Play the Harmonica

Begin by exploring your harmonica.
- Turn it over.
- Pick it up.
- Blow into it. Find the end with the *low* pitches.
- Hold the harmonica in your left hand with the *low* pitches to the *left*.

Now try this.
1. Put your mouth over the first lowest four holes.
   Hole 4 is C or tonal center.
   Holes 1–2–3 complete the chord under that melody tone.
2. Try blowing that chord. Does it sound good?
3. Before you begin to try a tune, try to play a scale.
   Beginning on C **(hole 4),** first *blow* into, then *draw* air out of *each* hole.
   Move your mouth to the right after you do this.
   Be sure you *blow* and *draw* over each hole.
   Did you find a spot where the scale did not sound right? At scale step 7, you have to *draw,* **then** *blow!*
4. Practice playing the **C scale** up and down until it sounds in tune and the *blow-draw* sequence is comfortable.
5. Try playing "Mary Had a Little Lamb" by ear.
   Begin by blowing into hole 5.

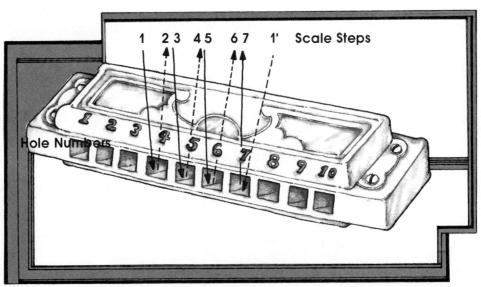

Play a Tune by Ear

Begin with a tune that you have heard so often you can hear it in your mind!
Get that tune "out of your head" and into the harmonica!
- Hunt for the tones, using trial and error.
- Keep trying until the tune moves smoothly.

Try playing a tune by ear. Then write it down.
Give it to other harmonica players.
Can they follow your "shorthand"?

Apply these helpful hints to the following familiar songs.

- Be sure you know the tune very well before trying to play it.
- Tune up by playing the scale on your harmonica.
- "Think" and hum the first pitch of the song, then try to match it on your harmonica. It will almost always require a *blow*, not a *draw*.
- As you play, try to think about the shape and direction of the tune.
    Does it go up or down?
    Does it move by steps or by skips?

Remember by Writing it Down.

Here is a sort of "shorthand" notation you might use. It shows the *hole numbers* to play, NOT the scale steps.
Uncircled numbers mean *blow.*
Circled numbers mean *draw.*

This is what "On Top of Old Smoky" would look like:

ON TOP OF OLD SMOKY

4   4   5   6   7   ⑥ ⑥ ⑤   6 ⑥   6
On top of Old Smok‑ey, All cov‑ered with snow,

4   4   5   6   6   ④ ④   5 ⑤ ④   4
I lost my true lov‑er, By court‑ing too slow.

Two Ways to Play the Harmonica

Full Chord Style:
You play 1 melody and 3 harmony pitches at the same time.
This is the style you have been practicing.

Single Note Style:
Only the melody pitch sounds. This is the style most harmonica players prefer.

Listen to this song. It is recorded in both styles.

DOWN IN THE VALLEY

Try playing in the single note style. To do this, place your mouth over the 4 holes as before. This time, let your tongue block the three holes to the *left*. This cuts off the air to the harmony pitches and allows only the melody pitch to sound.

Practice your **C scale** in this manner until it feels comfortable to sound only a single note. Do not get discouraged if it takes a while to learn to position your tongue correctly!

Can you read this harmonica "shorthand" and play in single note style?

3   4   ④   5   4   5   5   6   6   ④
Down in the val-ley, The val-ley so low,

3   ③   ④   6   6   ⑤   5   ④   4
Hang your head o-ver, Hear the wind blow

133

Add Vibrato

Vibrato adds the finishing touches to your harmonica playing. It is especially effective when used in the single note melody style. With your hands in the position shown below, simply wave at yourself with your right hand. You can control the vibrato by the speed of your wave. Vibrato is most often used on the long tones in slow tunes.

Play From Notation

This is what all the pitches of the ten-hole **C** harmonica look like on the musical staff:

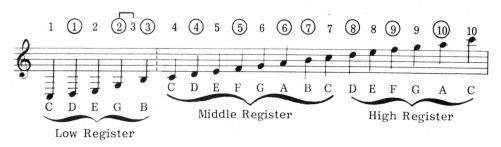

Follow the "shorthand" written above the staff on the next page. Learn to play "Polly Wolly Doodle," page 135. Ask someone to accompany you on guitar or washtub bass.

134

POLLY WOLLY DOODLE

American Folk Song

1. I___ went down South to___ see my Sal, sing-ing
2. Oh, a grass hop-per sit-ting on a rail-road track, Sing
3. Oh, I went to bed but it was-n't no use, Sing

pol-ly wol-ly doo-dle all the day; My___ Sal she is a___
pol-ly wol-ly doo-dle all the day; A - pick-ing his teeth with a
pol-ly wol-ly doo-dle all the day; My___ feet stuck out for a

spunk - y gal, sing-ing pol-ly wol-ly doo-dle all the day.
car - pet tack, Sing pol-ly wol-ly doo-dle all the day.
chick - en roost, Sing pol-ly wol-ly doo-dle all the day.

Chorus

Fare thee well, Fare thee well, Fare thee

well, my fair - y fey, For I'm goin' to Lou'-si-an-a for to

see my Su-si-an-na, sing-ing pol-ly wol-ly doo-dle all the day.

PUTTING ON THE STYLE

Traditional

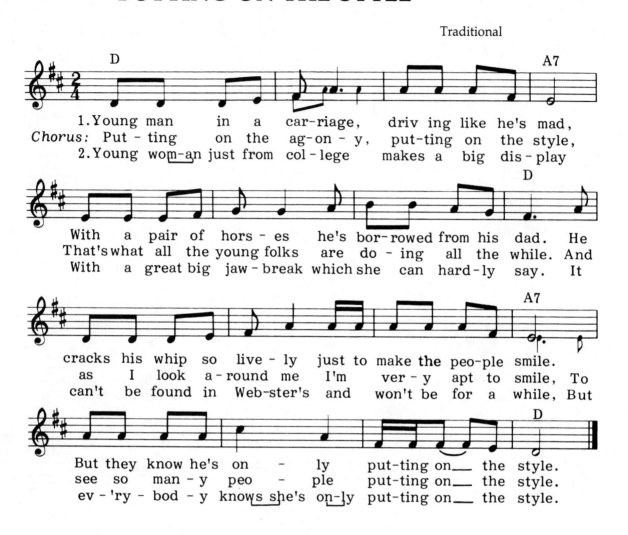

1. Young man in a car-riage, driv-ing like he's mad,
Chorus: Put-ting on the ag-on-y, put-ting on the style,
2. Young wom-an just from col-lege makes a big dis-play

With a pair of hors-es he's bor-rowed from his dad. He
That's what all the young folks are do-ing all the while. And
With a great big jaw-break which she can hard-ly say. It

cracks his whip so live-ly just to make the peo-ple smile.
as I look a-round me I'm ver-y apt to smile, To
can't be found in Web-ster's and won't be for a while, But

But they know he's on - ly put-ting on__ the style.
see so man-y peo - ple put-ting on__ the style.
ev-'ry-bod-y knows she's on-ly put-ting on__ the style.

TOM DOOLEY

Traditional

1. Hang down your head Tom Doo-ley, hang down your head and cry,
2. Take down my old vi-o-lin and play it all you please.
3. This world and one more and reck-on where I'd be.

Killed poor Lau-ra Fos-ter, you know you're bound to die.
At this time to-mor-row it'll be no use to me.
If it had-n't been for Gray-son, I'd a-been in Ten-nes-see.

SHADY GROVE

American Folk Song

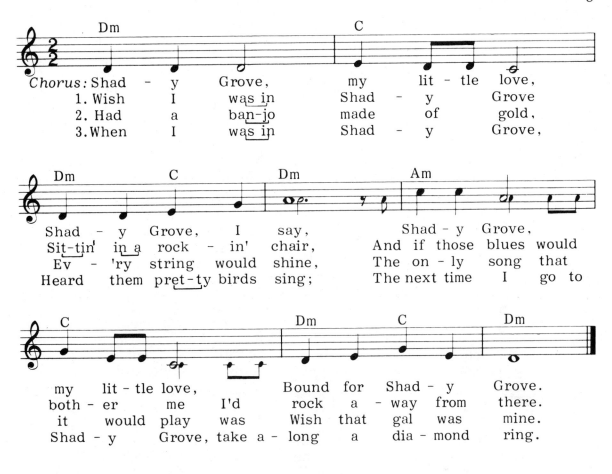

Chorus: Shad - y Grove, my lit - tle love,
1. Wish I was in Shad - y Grove
2. Had a ban-jo made of gold,
3. When I was in Shad - y Grove,

Shad - y Grove, I say, Shad - y Grove,
Sit-tin' in a rock - in' chair, And if those blues would
Ev - 'ry string would shine, The on - ly song that
Heard them pret-ty birds sing; The next time I go to

my lit - tle love, Bound for Shad - y Grove.
both - er me I'd rock a - way from there.
it would play was Wish that gal was mine.
Shad - y Grove, take a - long a dia - mond ring.

SIPPING CIDER THROUGH A STRAW

American Folk Song

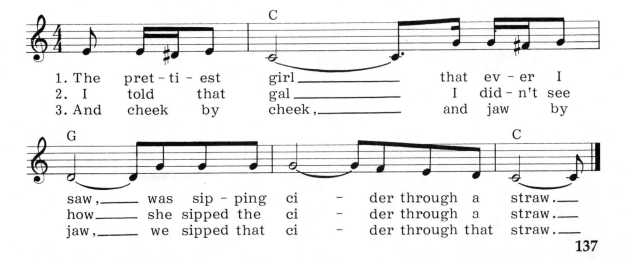

1. The pret - ti - est girl_____ that ev - er I
2. I told that gal_____ I did - n't see
3. And cheek by cheek,_____ and jaw by

saw,_____ was sip - ping ci - der through a straw._____
how_____ she sipped the ci - der through a straw._____
jaw,_____ we sipped that ci - der through that straw._____

137

TURKEY IN THE STRAW

Traditional

Verse

1. As I was a-go-ing down the road,
2. Oh, I went out to milk and I did-n't know how, I
3. Met Mis-ter Cat-fish com-in' down stream,
4. Came to the riv-er and I could-n't get a-cross,

Tired team and a heav-y load,
milked a goat in-stead of a cow, A
Says Mis-ter Cat-fish, "What does you mean?"
Paid five dol-lars for an old blind hoss.

Crack my whip and the lead-er sprung; I
mon-key sit-ting on a pile of straw, A-
Caught Mis-ter Cat-fish by the snout And
Would-n't go a-head nor he would-n't stand still, So he

says, "day-day" to the wag-on tongue.
wink-in' his eyes at his moth-er-in-law.
turned Mis-ter Cat-fish in-side out.
went up and down like an old saw-mill.

Chorus

Tur-key in the straw, (Instrumental or whistle)

tur-key in the hay, (Instrumental or whistle)

Roll 'em up and twist 'em up a high tuck-a-haw, And

hit 'em up a tune called "Tur-key in the straw!"

(GOOD OLD ELECTRIC) WASHING MACHINE (CIRCA 1943)

Words and Music
by John Hartford

Copyright © 1967 by Glaser Publications, Inc. Used with permission of the publisher.

ON TOP OF OLD SMOKY

Kentucky Folk Song

1. On top of old Smok - y_____ All cov - ered with snow,_____ I lost my true lov - er_____ By court - ing too slow._____
2. O court - ing's a pleas - ure,_____ But part-ing's a grief,_____ And a false heart - ed lov - er_____ Is worse than a thief._____
3. A thief will but rob you_____ Of all that you save,_____ But a false heart - ed lov - er_____ Sends you to the grave._____
4. The grave will de - cay you_____ And turn you to dust,_____ But a false heart - ed lov - er_____ You nev - er can trust._____

HARD, AIN'T IT HARD

American Folk Song

Moderately, in a 2 feeling

It's hard, and it's hard, ain't it hard_____ to love one who nev - er will love you._____ It's hard, and it's hard, ain't it hard, my old friend, to love one who nev - er will be true._____

OH, SUSANNA

by Stephen Foster

1. I___ come from Al - a - bam - a with a
   rained all night the day I left, the
3. I ___ had a dream the oth - er night when
   buck - wheat cake was in her mouth, the

ban - jo on my knee. I'm___ goin' to Lou' - si -
weath - er it was dry. The___ sun so hot I
ev - 'ry - thing was still. I___ thought I saw Su -
tear was in her eye. Says___ I, "I'm com - ing

an - a my Su - san - na for to see. 2. It__ cry.
froze to death Su - san - na don't you don't you cry.
san - na___ a - com - ing down the hill. 4. The_ cry.
from the South, Su - san - na, don't you cry.

Oh, Su - san - na, oh, don't you cry for me, For I

come from Al - a - bam - a with a ban - jo on my knee.

Playing the Guitar

Tuning Pegs

Nut

Frets

Head

Fingerboard

Sound Hole

Neck

Bridge

Body

Assume responsibility
for learning the guitar.
Begin within the large group,
then continue at your own pace.
Ask questions when you need help.

Playing Position

Hold your guitar comfortably and securely. The correct body position is important so that no effort or energy is wasted when playing.

Raise your left foot by placing it on a stool or coffee can. Place the guitar so that there are four points of contact with your body:

1) underneath the right forearm;
2) against the chest;
3) inside the right thigh;
4) on the left knee.

If you are holding the guitar correctly, your right hand will fall directly in front of you.

Your body should be aligned vertically, with your shoulders level. Slant the guitar so that its head is slightly higher than your shoulders.

Hand Positions

Left Hand

- Practice the correct left-hand position by touching the thumb to the middle finger. Apply pressure. Observe how the thumb provides a balance point in this position for all fingers.
- Place the thumb on the back of the guitar neck to provide balance and support for the fingers pressing down on the strings.
- Press with fingertips to avoid touching adjacent strings.
- Left-hand fingers are numbered as shown.

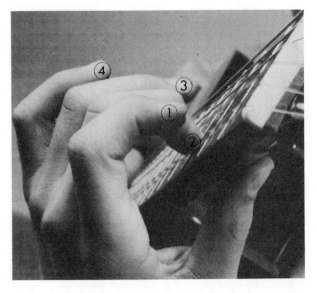

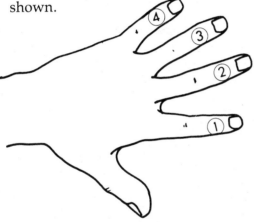

Right Hand

- Place the right hand in a relaxed manner just behind the sound hole.
- Chords may be strummed by brushing the thumb from the lowest to the highest string.
- The thumb and fingers may also be used independently to pluck individual strings.

Strum a Chord

C CHORD (four strings)

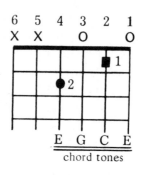

E G C E
chord tones

O means "open string"
X means "do not strum"

Press firmly on the strings with your left-hand fingers. Place the thumb behind the middle finger (②) to provide support.

Play this "short" **C** chord. Strum only the four highest strings: 4 3 2 1.

The numbers on the chord chart tell you which fingers to use.

The **root** of the chord is shown by a □.
Other pitches are shown by a ○.

Practice strumming the **C** chord.

Sing these familiar rounds as you strum the **C** chord.
- "Row, Row, Row Your Boat" (begin singing on C).
- "Three Blind Mice" (begin singing on E).

144

Move to a New Chord

G7 CHORD (four strings)

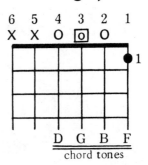

6	5	4	3	2	1
X	X	O	🔲	O	●1

D G B F
chord tones

To find the **G7** chord, play **C,** then roll
your index finger back to the first string.
All other fingers are off the strings.
Strum only the four highest strings.

Practice moving between the **C** and **G7** chords until you find them easily.

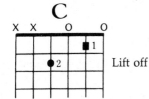

C

Lift off

G7

Roll back to
String 1

STRUM:

POLLY WOLLY DOODLE

American Folk Song

- Strum C chord.
- Pluck for beginning C pitch.

    C /   /
Oh, I went down South to see my Sal,

      /   **G7** /
Sing Pol-ly wol-ly doo-dle all the day;

      /   /
My Sal-ly is a spunk-y gal,

      /   **C** /
Sing Pol-ly wol-ly doo-dle all the day.

      /   /
Fare thee well, fare thee well,

      /   **G7** /
Fare thee well, my fair-y fay,

      /   /
For I'm going to Loui-si-an-a, for to see my Su-sy-an-na,

      /   **C** /
Sing Pol-ly wol-ly doo-dle all the day.

Using Five and Six Strings

C CHORD (five strings)

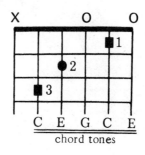

C E G C E
chord tones

Strum this five-string **C** chord. It sounds
better than the four-string **C** chord
because the root of the chord is now the
lowest sound.

Play the songs you have just learned using this new chord position.
Then learn to accompany "Blow the Man Down."

BLOW THE MAN DOWN

- Strum **C** chord.
- Pluck C for beginning pitch.

Sea Chantey

Come_ all ye young fel-lows that fol-low the sea, with a

Yeo - Ho, blow the man down! And please pay at-ten-tion and

lis-ten to me. Give us some time to blow the man down.

G7 CHORD (six strings)

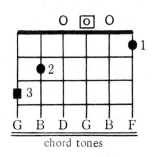

G B D G B F
chord tones

Using the Buddy System

Play "Polly Wolly Doodle" (page 145) with a friend. You play only the **C** chord. Your friend plays only the **G7** chord. Do not play the guitar when it is your friend's turn. Both of you should sing the melody.

Example:

                 C *(you play . . .)*

Oh, I went down South to see my Sal,

                                   G7 *(friend plays . . .)*

Sing Pol-ly wol-ly doo-dle all the day;

My Sal-ly is a spunk-y gal, . . .

- Learn to move from the five-string **C** chord to the six-string **G7** chord.

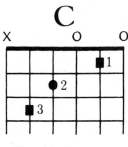

- Play this **C** chord

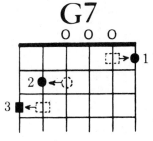

- Spread each finger wider by one string to move from C to G7.

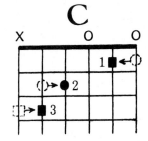

- Move each finger together by one string to move from G7 to C.

Strum the five highest strings for **C** and all six strings for **G7**. Practice this chord change many times. Then play the songs you know that use these chords.

Play Root Bass

Listen to the recording of "Guantanamera." After you are familiar with the melody, add a *guitarrón* part. The *guitarrón* is a large, round-bottomed bass guitar used in *mariachi* bands. It is plucked by the performer.

Root Bass

Play only the root of each chord on the two lowest strings of the guitar. This three-note pattern repeats throughout the song.

Note names: F   Bb   C

Make sure your guitar is in tune with the recording. Then add your root-bass part to the sounds of the mariachi musicians.

GUANTANAMERA

(Lady of Guantanamo)

Original lyrics and music
by José Fernandez Días
(Joseito Fernandez)
Based on a poem by José Martí

Spanish words by José Martí

	F	Bb	C		F	Bb	C

REFRAIN: Guan - ta - na - mer - a, gua - ji - ra Guan - ta - na - mer - a.

           F   Bb C   F   Bb C

Guan - ta - na - mer - a, gua - ji - ra Guan - ta - na - mer - a.

                 F   Bb   C

VERSE: Yo soy un hom - bre sin - ce - ro

                    F   Bb   C

De don - de cre - ce la pal - ma,___

                    F   Bb   C

Yo soy un hom - bre sin - ce - ro,

                  F Bb   C

De don - de cre - ce la pal - ma,

                   F   Bb C

Y an - tes de mor - rir -me quie - ro,

                   F   Bb C

E - char mis ver - sos del al - ma.

REFRAIN

© Copyright 1963, 1965 by FALL RIVER MUSIC, INC. All rights reserved. Used by permission.

Finger Placement Pitch Chart

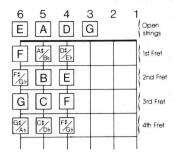

- Learn to play a bass part for "Spinning Wheel."
- Use the **Finger Placement Pitch Chart** to find the root of the chords.
- Notice that the song has four sections, three of which are almost the same.
- Tune your guitar and play with the recording.

SPINNING WHEEL

Arr. B.A.R.   Words and Music by David C. Thomas

E(7)   A(7) D(7)   G
What goes up must come down,

E(7)   A(7) D(7)   G
Spin - ning Wheel got to go 'round.

E(7)   A(7)   D(7)   G
Talk - in' 'bout your trou - bles is a cry - in' sin, . . .

D(7)   D(7)
Ride a paint - ed po - ny, let the Spin - ning Wheel _____ spin.

E(7)   A(7)   D(7)   G
You got no mon - ey, you got no home, _____

E(7)   A(7) D(7)   G
Spin - ning Wheel all a - lone, _____

E(7)   A(7)   D(7)   G
Talk - in' 'bout your trou - bles and you, you nev - er learn, _____

D(7)   D(7)
Ride a paint - ed po - ny, let the Spin - ning Wheel _____ turn.

C   Bb
Did you find your di - rect - ing sign _____

          Ab   G
On the straight and nar - row high - way? _____

C   Bb
Would you mind _____ a re - flect - ing sign? _____

          Ab   G
Just let it shine _____ with - in your mind, _____

          G   Bb   C   D
And show you _____ the col - ors _____ that are real. _____

E(7)   A(7)   D(7)   G
Some - one is wait - ing just for you, _____

E(7)   D(7)   G
Spin - ning Wheel spin - ning true, _____

E(7)   A(7)   D(7)   G
Drop all your trou - bles by the riv - er - side, _____

D(7)
Catch a paint - ed po - ny on the Spin - ning Wheel _____ ride.

© Copyright 1968 by Blackwood Music, Inc. and Bay Music Ltd. Used by permission. All rights reserved.

FROG WENT A-COURTIN'

Traditional

Learn the **D CHORD.** Strum it on the first beat of each measure.

• Begin singing on D.

1. Frog went a-court-in' and he did ride, uh - huh (uh-
rode right_ to_____ Miss Mous-ie's door, uh - huh (uh-
took Miss_ Mous - ie on his knee, uh - huh (uh-

huh), A frog went a-court-in' and he did ride, uh huh (uh-
huh), He rode right_ to_____ Miss Mous-ie's door, uh huh (uh-
huh), He took Miss_ Mous - ie on his knee, uh huh (uh-

huh), A frog went a court-in' and he did ride, A
huh), He rode right_ to_____ Miss Mous - ie's door, Where
huh), He took Miss_ Mous - ie on his knee,

sword and pis - tol by his side, uh - huh._____ 2. He
he had of - ten been be-fore, uh - huh._____ 3. He
Said, "Miss Mous-ie will you mar-ry me, uh - huh."_____

4. "Without my Uncle Rat's consent,"
    uh - huh (Uh-huh),
  "I couldn't marry the president!"
    uh - huh.

5. Uncle Rat gave his consent,
    uh - huh (uh - huh),
  So they got married and off they
  went,
    uh - huh.

PUTTING ON THE STYLE

A7 CHORD

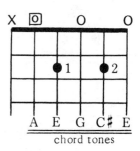

A E G C♯ E
chord tones

Learn the **A7** chord and the melody for "Putting on the Style" (page 136). Use the **D** and **A7** chords to accompany yourself as you sing.

    D   **A(7)**
Put - ting on the a - gon - y, put - ting on the style,

                                                D
That's what all the young folks are do - ing all the while.

                                    A(7)
And as I look a - round me, I'm very apt to smile,

                                    D
To see so man - y peo - ple put - ting on the style.

Learn to Tune Your Guitar

One way to tune the guitar is by matching the strings to the sounds of the piano or a pitch pipe.

Ask for help when first learning to tune the guitar.

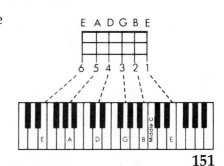

TALKING GUITAR BLUES

by Ernest Tubbs

Follow the words of this Talking Blues as you listen to the recording by John Berry.

Now you wanta get in trouble, here's how you do it
You just git a guitar and you're in to it.
'Cause you play all day and you play all night
And your folks tell you'll never learn to git it right
Always fussing ____ naggin' ____
Try to run you down to the hen house.

Well, I bought a guitar 'bout a year ago
And the feller said, I'd learn it in a week or so
And he gimmie a little pick and a book or two,
Said, "There ya are, John, it's up to you!"
Dirty dog ____ Cost me $4.95, ever cent of money I had
Over time money, too!

Well, none the less, I'd spent my dough
And couldn't let it go to the waste, ya know.
So, I took that book and guitar and all
And headed off home where the grass grows tall.
Way high up there in Brixton.
Good place to be if you got a guitar.
Sure is awful if ya ain't.

Well, I played all day and I played all night
And I could see Ma's hair was a-turning white
And her face all lined with discontent
And I knew her patience was gitten' spent
She's kinda nervous ____ agitated ____ ears ringin'.

And my sister took it the worst of all
'Cause she got married that coming fall.
She says, "for love," I got my doubts!
I reckon this guitar drove her out.
She's a game gal, ____ just couldn't take it
____
Well, there's a limit to everythin'.

Now my Pa he took it in a different way
He said, "Son you might turn your Ma's hair gray
And drive your sisters away from home,
But you or me, boys, are gonna roam.
And I ain't leavin. Never intended to ____
figure it out!" I did.

So the very next day my clothes git packed;
Slung that guitar across my back
And I gits me aboard on a long freight train.
Search the world for my share of fame.
Ain't found any ____ heartaches ____ Mayfair Hotel ____ handouts.

G CHORD (four strings)

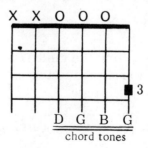

X X O O O

3

D G B G
chord tones

- Learn the four-string **G** chord.
- Make up your own Talking Blues.
- Use this chord sequence:

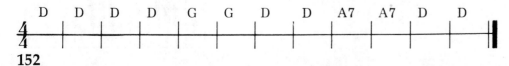

| D | D | D | D | G | G | D | D | A7 | A7 | D | D |

Listen to Folk-Rock Guitar

COLOR HIM FOLKY

by Howard Roberts

Follow this chart as you listen to music performed by a 12-string guitar and ensemble.

1

A (**minor** tonality)

Introduction: syncopated vamp . . .

$\frac{4}{4}$ ♩ ♩ ♫ ♪ | ♩ ♫ ♫ ♫ | leads into the first tune.

Rhythm guitars **STOP** suddenly with an accented strum

Melody continues.

Ascending chords move to a new modality.

2

B (**major** tonality)

Continuous driving rhythm accompanies new tune,

then another **STOP**

Low walking bass leads into the next section.

3

A Back to **minor** tonality.

First idea repeated; melody slightly varied.

4

B **Major** tonality.

"B" idea repeated.

5

A Theme returns, but is not completed.

Gradually fades out.

Bottleneck Guitar

The guitar can be tuned in special ways for different styles of playing. To play bottleneck guitar, the strings are tuned to form a **G** major chord when strummed in open position.

Try tuning your guitar like this. If necessary, ask for help in retuning your guitar strings to the correct pitches.

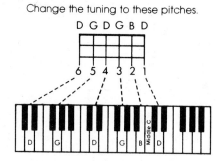

Change the tuning to these pitches.

Play Bottleneck Guitar

A bottleneck guitar player slides a glass bottle neck or metal cylinder up and down the fingerboard to change the chords.

Use a cylinder on your left ring finger (③). Slide your covered finger up and down to change chords.

Play the I – IV – V Chord Pattern

I (G Chord) –strum open strings
IV (C Chord) – move the cylinder to the fifth fret
V (D Chord) – move the cylinder to the seventh fret

THIS TRAIN

American Folk Song

Listen to the bottleneck guitar in "This Train." As the guitarist slides up and down the fret board, you will hear the bottleneck bend and change the guitar's pitches.

WORRIED MAN BLUES

American Folk Song

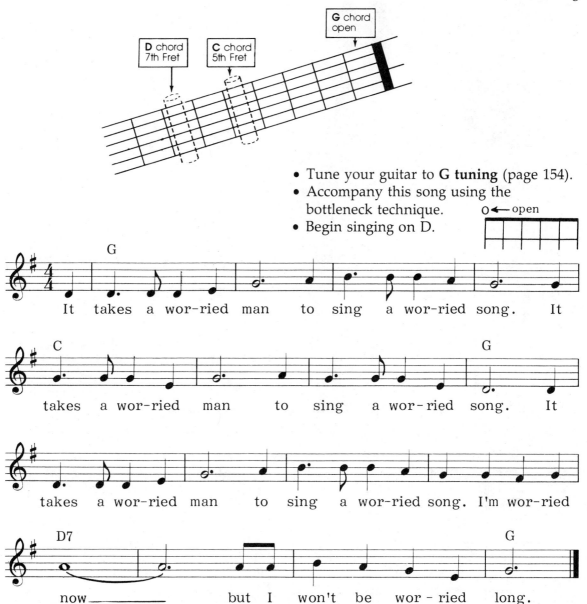

- Tune your guitar to **G tuning** (page 154).
- Accompany this song using the bottleneck technique.
- Begin singing on D.

G

It takes a wor-ried man to sing a wor-ried song. It

C ... **G**

takes a wor-ried man to sing a wor-ried song. It

takes a wor-ried man to sing a wor-ried song. I'm wor-ried

D7 ... **G**

now _____ but I won't be wor-ried long.

Use this same tuning and playing style to accompany an early rock song.

REELIN' AND ROCKIN' (page 7)

Listen and play along with the recording. Your ear should tell you when to change the chord.

CHORD SEQUENCE: G   C   G   D   C   G

155

Play Minor Chords

Em CHORD

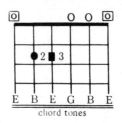

E B E G B E
chord tones

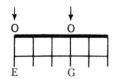

E   G

- Accompany this song with one chord.
Try out various strumming and plucking patterns.

- Begin singing the Melody on G; the Chant on E.

ZUM GALI GALI

Israeli Work Song

(Melody)

1. He - cha - lutz   l' - maan   a - vo - dah;_____
2. A - vo - dah   l' - maan   he - cha - lutz;_____
3. He - cha - lutz   l' - maan   ha - b'tu - lah;_____
4. Ha - sha - lom   l' - maan   ha - 'a - mim;_____

Chant

Zum   ga - li   ga - li   ga - li,   Zum   ga - li   ga - li,

___   A - vo - dah   l' - maan   he - cha - lutz.
___   He - cha - lutz   l' - maan   a - vo - dah.
___   Ha - b'tu - lah   l' - maan   he - cha - lutz.
___   Ha - 'a - mim   l' - maan   ha - sha - lom.

Zum   ga - li   ga - li   ga - li,   Zum   ga - li   ga - li.

Transpose "Zum Gali Gali" to the key of
A minor. Use the **A minor** chord throughout.

Now play it in the key of **D minor.** Use
the **D minor** chord throughout.

- Which key is the most comfortable
range for your voice?

Am CHORD

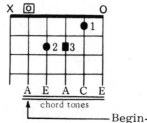

A E A C E
chord tones

Dm CHORD

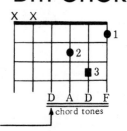

D A D F
chord tones

Begin

156

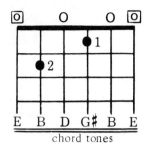

- Practice moving between **Am** and **Dm**.
- Learn the **E7** chord.
- Then sing and play this blues song.
- Begin singing on A.

DEEP FORK RIVER BLUES

Words and music by Tom Paxton

1. Now the Deep Fork is a mud-dy riv-er ____ near my home, ____ near my home. ____ Yes, the Deep Fork is a mud-dy riv-er ____ near my home, near my home.
2. Now the Deep Fork is in Ok-la-hom-a ____ near my home, ____ near my home. ____ Yes, the Deep Fork is in Ok-la-hom-a ____ near my home, near my home.
3. I can hear hounds bay-ing on the riv-er ____ near my home, ____ near my home. ____ And I'll sure-ly have a rab-bit for my din-ner ____ near my home, near my home.

4. When the sun goes down a man gets
   awful lonesome
   For his home, for his home.
   When the sun goes down a man gets
   awful lonesome
   For his home, for his home.

5. Well, I don't have to stay away
   forever
   I can go home, I can go home.
   No, I don't have to stay away
   forever
   I can go home, I can go home.

© Copyright 1962 Cherry Lane Music Co. Used by permission. All rights reserved.

Slide and Pivot from Chord to Chord

G CHORD (six strings)

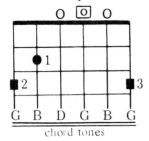

G B D G B G
chord tones

D7 CHORD

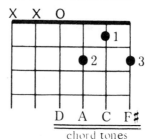

D A C F♯
chord tones

G

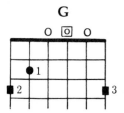

Move to D7 from G

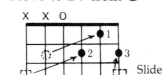

Slide

Move to C from D7

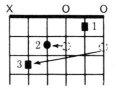

Use "1" as a pivot. Swing other fingers into position for **C**.

• Begin singing on G.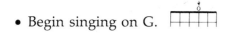

MAMA DON'T 'LOW

Traditional

1. Ma - ma don't 'low no gui - tar pick - in' 'round here._____
2. Ma - ma don't 'low no ban - jo play - in' 'round here._____
3. Ma - ma don't 'low no cig - ar smok - in' 'round here._____
4. Ma - ma don't 'low no mid - night ram - blin' 'round here._____

Ma - ma don't 'low no gui - tar pick - in' 'round here._____
Ma - ma don't 'low no ban - jo play - in' 'round here._____
Ma - ma don't 'low no cig - ar smok - in' 'round here._____
Ma - ma don't 'low no mid - night ram - blin' 'round here._____

I don't care what Ma - ma don't 'low, Gon - na pick my gui - tar
I don't care what Ma - ma don't 'low, Gon - na play my ban - jo
I don't care what Ma - ma don't 'low, Gon - na smoke my cig - ar
I don't care what Ma - ma don't 'low, Gon na ram ble at mid - night

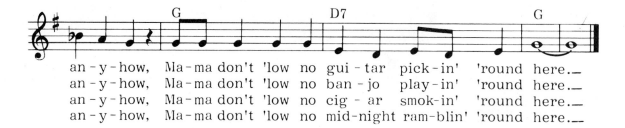

an-y-how,	Ma-ma don't 'low	no	gui-tar	pick-in'	'round here.—
an-y-how,	Ma-ma don't 'low	no	ban-jo	play-in'	'round here.—
an-y-how,	Ma-ma don't 'low	no	cig-ar	smok-in'	'round here.—
an-y-how,	Ma-ma don't 'low	no	mid-night ram-blin'	'round here.—

...No Skiffle-Band Playin' 'Round Here

Sing new words to "Mama Don't 'Low"

**Mama don't 'low no skiffle-band playin' 'round here.
Mama don't 'low no skiffle-band playin' 'round here.
I don't care what Mama don't 'low,
Gonna play in a skiffle-band anyhow.
Mama don't 'low no skiffle-band playin' 'round here.**

Add the sounds of the Skiffle Band to the guitar accompaniment.
- **Kazoo–Comb:** play the melody or improvise a harmony part.
- **Spoons–Washboard–Limberjack:** improvise rhythms; create special effects.
- **Washtub Bass–Jugs:** play root bass harmony.
- **Mouthbow:** play the melody or make up a harmony part.

Repeat the song several times. Alternate singing with improvised solos by skiffle-band performers.

Tune the Guitar Using Relative Tuning

1. Place the 2nd finger of your left hand on the 5th fret of the low E string (6).
2. Pluck that string.
3. Then pluck the next highest string (5), the *open* A.
4. Do the sounds match?
   - If they do not, adjust the open A string.
   - If the sounds match, continue the same process by following the diagram until you have tuned all six strings.

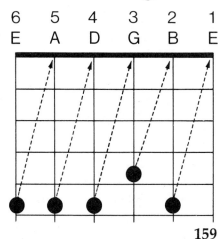

159

Unit IV
THE CHORAL-SINGING EXPERIENCE

CHART 18: Commitment to Musical Learning (5)	
In this section you will have an opportunity to participate in the choral-singing experience . . .	
interpret and perform music in an appropriate style	sing expressively by relating lyrics and musical settings
train your ear to sing in tune with others	analyze choral-arranging devices
sing using good choral techniques	perform different vocal parts

- Which of these can you now do independently?
- In which areas will you commit yourself to becoming more independent?

I WRITE THE SONGS

Arranged by Buryl Red

Words and Music by Bruce Johnston

Study the score. Which parts of this arrangement can you sing most comfortably? Work with others and plan a vocal performance.

I've been a - live for - ev - er,

and I wrote the ver - y first song.

I put the words and the mel - o - dies to - geth - er, I am

mu - sic, and I write the songs.

I write the songs that make the whole world sing;

I write the songs of love and spe - cial things.

I write the songs that make the young girls cry;

1. I write the songs, I write the songs. **2.**

I am mu - sic, and I write the songs.

Copyright © 1974 by Artists Music, Inc. This arrangement copyright © 1981 by Artists Music, Inc. All rights throughout the world administered by INTERWORLD MUSIC GROUP, INC. 8304 Beverly Boulevard, Los Angeles, CA 90048. Used by permission. All rights reserved.

SKIP TO MY LOU

Arranged by Buryl Red   American Singing Game

Listen to the three patterns shown below. Discuss the similarities and differences in the way they sound and in the way they are notated.

Changing Voices and **Baritones** will need to be able to read parts notated in various ways.

- Sometimes **Changing Voices** and **Baritones** will read a part notated in the treble clef but will sing an octave lower than written. This could be shown with this symbol: *8va*.
- Sometimes the **Changing Voice** part will be notated in the treble clef and at the notated pitch.
- Sometimes **Changing Voice** and **Baritone** parts will be notated in the bass clef and sung at the notated pitch.

For this song, your parts are identified in two ways. For the *Verse*, the numbers in the margin indicate that you may choose your part. Will **Baritones** and **Changing Voices** sing at notated pitch or an octave lower?

For the *Refrain*, sing your specified part. Will **Changing Voices** sing at notated pitch or an octave lower? What about the **Baritones?**

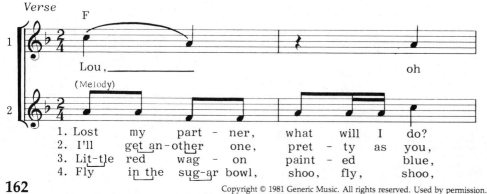

          Copyright © 1981 Generic Music. All rights reserved. Used by permission.

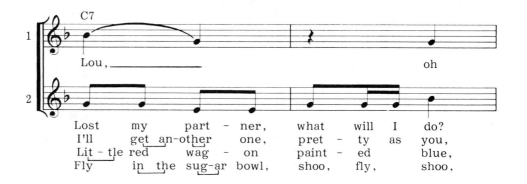

Lou, _____ oh

Lost my part - ner, what will I do?
I'll get an-other one, pret - ty as you,
Lit - tle red wag - on paint - ed blue,
Fly in the sug-ar bowl, shoo, fly, shoo,

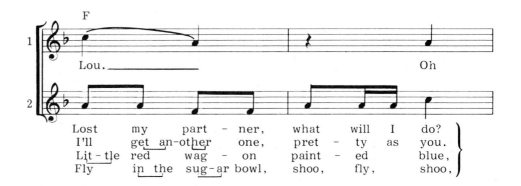

Lou. _____ Oh

Lost my part - ner, what will I do?
I'll get an-other one, pret - ty as you.
Lit - tle red wag - on paint - ed blue,
Fly in the sug-ar bowl, shoo, fly, shoo,

skip, _____ my dar - ling.

Skip to my Lou, my dar - ling.

Refrain

Tr. I

Skip, skip, skip to my Lou, Skip, skip,

Tr. II

Skip, oh skip, my Lou, Skip, oh skip,

C.V.

Lou, _____ oh Lou, _____

Bar.

Skip, my Lou, oh__ skip, my

163

TEAR DOWN THE WALLS

Arranged by Buryl Red

Words and Music by Fred Nell

TRO–© Copyright 1964 & 1965 Folkways Music Publishers, Inc., New York, N.Y. Used by permission.

The mu - sic's ev - 'ry - where,_ wher - ev - er
man is free,_ The mu - sic's in the air_ that
lights the road_ to lib - er - ty.

Tr. I   walls._

Tr. II   sing._   Ring and sing.

C.V.   sing._   Ring and sing.

Bar.   sing._   Ring and sing.

* Sing in unison. Tr. I, Tr. II, and Bar. sing at pitch; C.V. sings an octave lower than written.

EASE ON DOWN THE ROAD

Arranged by Buryl Red

Words and music by Charlie Smalls

Around which notes does the melody seem to center during the Refrain? the Verse? What effect does this change have on the expressive character of music?

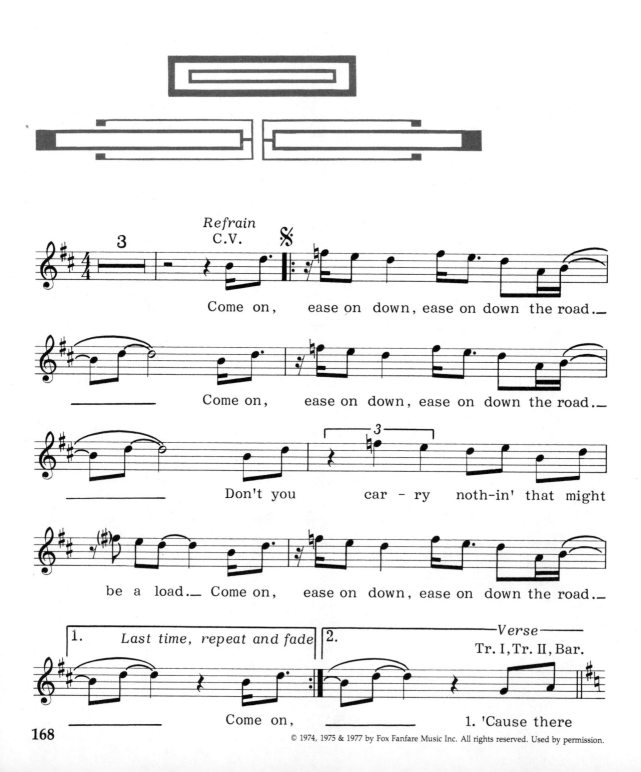

Refrain
C.V.

Come on, ease on down, ease on down the road._

Come on, ease on down, ease on down the road._

Don't you car - ry noth-in' that might

be a load._ Come on, ease on down, ease on down the road._

1. *Last time, repeat and fade*

2. Verse
Tr. I, Tr. II, Bar.

Come on, ____ 1. 'Cause there

© 1974, 1975 & 1977 by Fox Fanfare Music Inc. All rights reserved. Used by permission.

may be times— when you think you've lost your mind— and the
left foot up—— when your right—— one's down.—— Come on

steps you've ta - ken leave you three, four steps be-hind.— Just you
legs, keep mov-in', don't you lose—— no ground,—'cause the

keep on keep - in' on the road that you choose and don't
road you're walk - in' might be long some - time, but just

1.
give up walk - in' 'cause you gave up— shoes.— 2. Pick your
keep on step - in' and you'll

Refrain
C.V.
only
2.
3
D.S.
be just— fine.—
Come on,

HURDY GURDY MAN

Arranged by Buryl Red

Words and Music by Donovan Leitch

Work for clear, crisp diction as you perform these lyrics.
Observe how the musical rhythm reflects the natural
rhythm of the words.

Steadily droning on

Oh _____

1. Thrown like a star in my __ vast sleep I
2. His - to - ries __ of ag - es past __

o - pen my eyes __ to take __ a peep __
un - en - light - ened __ shad - ows cast __

To find __ that I __ was by __ the sea, __
Down __ through all __ e - ter - ni - ty, __ the

gaz - ing with tran - quil - i - ty. __ 'Twas
cry - ing of hu - man - i - ty. __ 'Tis

then when the Hur - dy Gur - dy Man __ came
then when the Hur - dy Gur - dy Man __ comes

sing - ing songs of love, _____ Then when the Hur - dy Gur - dy Man __ came
sing - ing songs of love, _____ Then when the Hur - dy Gur - dy Man __ comes

170

Copyright © 1968 by Donovan (Music) Ltd. Sole selling agent Peer International Corporation. Used by permission.

sing - ing songs _____ of love. _____
sing - ing songs _____ of love. _____

Hur - dy gur - dy hur - dy gur - dy hur - dy gur - dy, gur - dy he sang, _____

Hur - dy gur - dy hur - dy gur - dy hur - dy gur - dy, gur - dy he sang, _____

D.C.

Hur - dy gur - dy hur - dy gur - dy hur - dy gur - dy, gur - dy he sang, _____

Hur - dy gur - dy hur - dy gur - dy hur - dy gur - dy, gur - dy he sang, _____

Here comes the ro - ly po - ly man ___ and he's sing - ing songs of love, _____

Repeat and fade

Ro - ly po - ly ro - ly po - ly, po - ly ro - ly po - ly he sang. _____

A PLACE IN THE SUN

Lyrics by Ronald Miller
Arranged by Buryl Red

Music by Bryan Wells

Read the lyrics aloud. How do the word-sounds help express the mood?
Experiment with ways of performing the song that will show the relationship between word-sound and meaning.

Copyright © 1966 Jobete Music Company, Inc. Used by permission.

DELTA DAWN

Arranged by Lowell Rogers

Words and Music by Alex Harvey
and Larry Collins

Can you identify one or two popular music styles that have influenced this song?

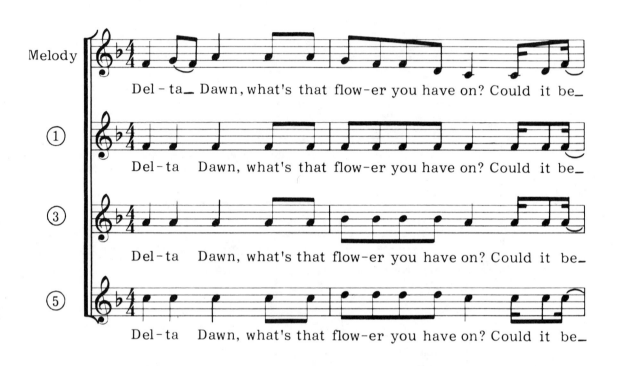

Melody: Del - ta_ Dawn, what's that flow-er you have on? Could it be_

① Del - ta Dawn, what's that flow-er you have on? Could it be_

③ Del - ta Dawn, what's that flow-er you have on? Could it be_

⑤ Del - ta Dawn, what's that flow-er you have on? Could it be_

Mel.: ___ a fad - ed rose from days gone by? And

① ___ a fad - ed rose from days gone by? And

③ ___ a fad - ed rose from days gone by? And

⑤ ___ a fad - ed rose from days gone by? And

did I hear you say he was a-meet-in' you here to-day____ to

did I hear you say he was a-meet-in' you here to-day____ to

did I hear you say he was a-meet-in' you here to-day____ to

did I hear you say he was a-meet-in' you here to-day____ to

take you to his man-sion in the sky?

take you to his man-sion in the sky?

take you to his man-sion in the sky?

take you to his man-sion in the sky?

GONNA GET ALONG WITHOUT YOU NOW

Arranged by Buryl Red

Words and Music by Milton Kellem

Got a-long with-out_ ya be-fore I met_ ya, gon-na get a-long with-out ya now._ Gon-na find some-bod-y twice as cute_ 'cause ya did-n't love me an-y how._ You ran a-round_ with ev-'ry Ooh_ girl in town_ and ya nev-er cared_ if it got me down._ You had me wor-ried, al-ways Oh._ on my guard,_ But ya laughed at me_ 'cause I

Copyright © 1952 Bibo Music Publishers. Copyright renewed. International copyright secured.
All rights reserved. Used by permission.

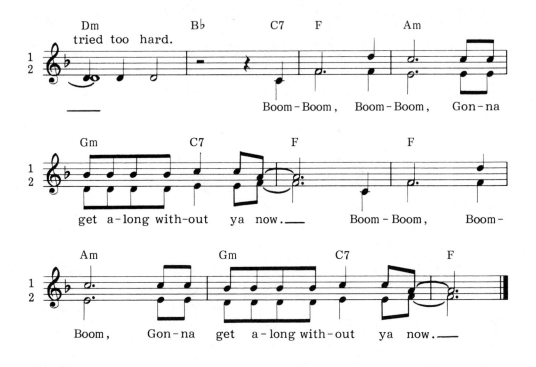

SPINNING WHEEL

Arranged by Buryl Red

Words and Music by David C. Thomas

Study the score. Notice the following.

- Emphasis on the half-step interval, such as B to C.
- Sections whose parts move in parallel motion; in contrary motion.
- Repeated melodic and rhythmic patterns.

Discuss expressive reasons for using these musical devices.

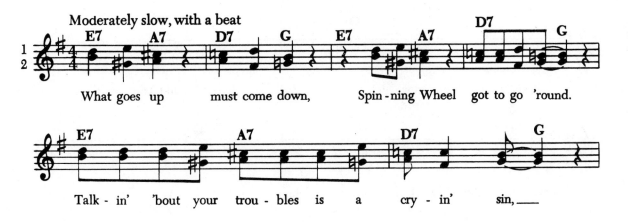

© Copyright 1968 by Blackwood Music, Inc. and Bay Music Ltd. Used by permission. All rights reserved.

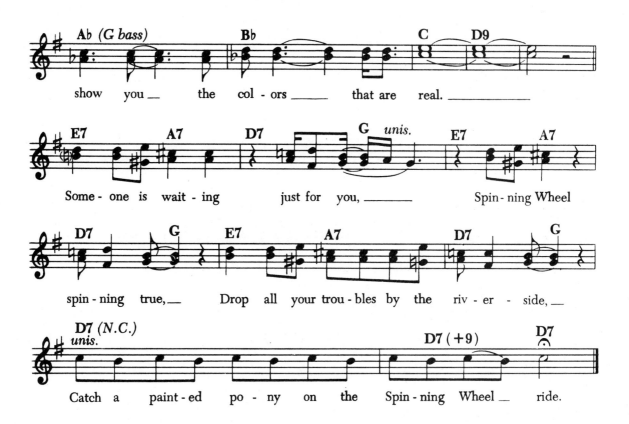

show you __ the col - ors __ that are real. _____

Some - one is wait - ing just for you, _____ Spin - ning Wheel spin - ning true, __ Drop all your trou - bles by the riv - er - side, __ Catch a paint - ed po - ny on the Spin - ning Wheel __ ride.

Develop your own rock accompaniment for "Spinning Wheel." This chord progression may be played throughout the song.

Develop an introduction similar to that on the recording. Use this pattern. Instruments enter one at a time.

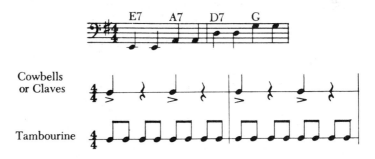

Develop a coda similar to that on the recording.

GO DOWN MOSES

Arranged by Buryl Red

Spiritual

180

Copyright © 1971 by Buryl A. Red. All rights reserved. Used by permission.

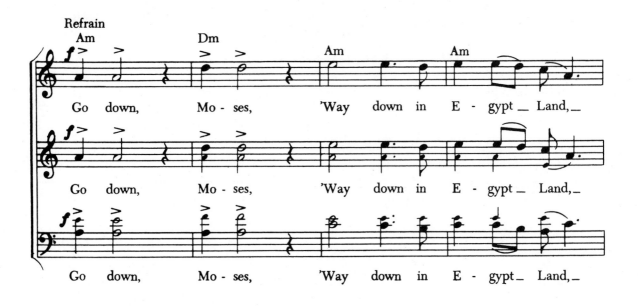

Go down, Moses, 'Way down in E - gypt — Land, —

Go down, Moses, 'Way down in E - gypt — Land, —

Go down, Moses, 'Way down in E - gypt — Land, —

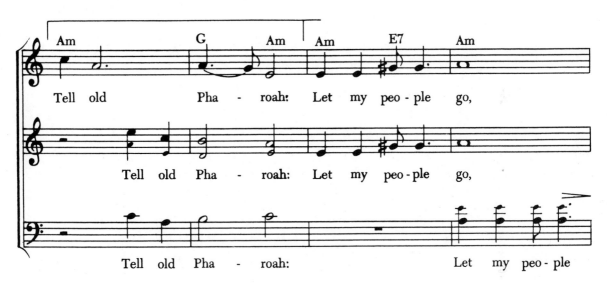

Tell old Pha - roah: Let my peo - ple go,

Tell old Pha - roah: Let my peo - ple go,

Tell old Pha - roah: Let my peo - ple

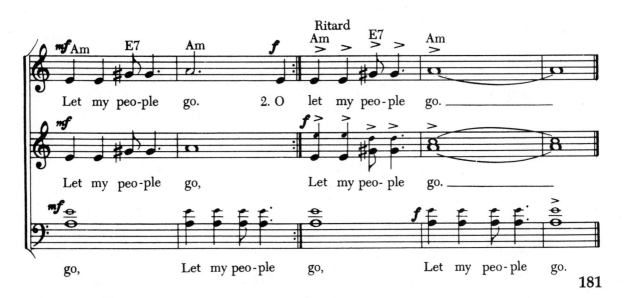

Let my peo - ple go. 2. O let my peo - ple go. —

Let my peo - ple go, Let my peo - ple go. —

go, Let my peo - ple go, Let my peo - ple go.

Guantanamera
(Lady of Guantanamo)

Based on a poem by José Marti

Original lyrics and music
by José Fernandez Dias
(Joseito Fernandez)

Copyright © 1963, 1965 by FALL RIVER MUSIC, INC. All rights reserved. Used by permission.

This song, like "Spinning Wheel," is based on an **harmonic ostinato.**

Guitar and autoharp players may make up patterns such as these:

The root notes of the chord progression make a bass line.

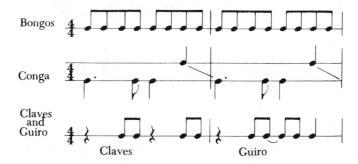

Make up patterns with percussion instruments.

A few voices may sing this vocal ostinato during all or part of the song.

Vocal Ostinato

Guan - ta - na - mer- a

The literal translation of the Spanish is as follows:

I'm a sincere man from the land of palms. Before dying, I wish
to pour forth the poems of my soul.

My verses are soft green but also a flaming red. My verses are
like wounded fauns seeking refuge in the forest.

I want to share my fate with the world's humble. A little mountain stream pleases me more than the ocean.

SCARBOROUGH FAIR

Arranged by Fred Bock

English Folk Song

Copyright © 1969 by Gentry Publications, Tarzana, California. International Copyright Secured.
All rights reserved. Used by permission.

A variety of dynamics are included in this song. Put them in order from softest to loudest. Practice controlling your voice as you move from one dynamic level to the next.

WHEN I'M SIXTY-FOUR

Arranged by Buryl Red

Words and Music by John Lennon
and Paul McCartney

Before you begin to sing, study the score carefully. It will make learning the song easier and quicker. Begin by identifying the sections. What are the distinctive characteristics of each? How do these characteristics contribute to the musical expressiveness of the song?

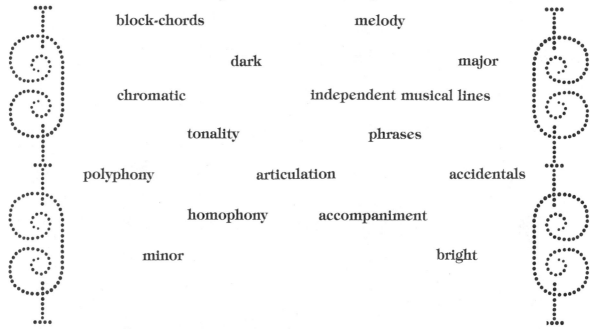

block-chords   melody

dark   major

chromatic   independent musical lines

tonality   phrases

polyphony   articulation   accidentals

homophony   accompaniment

minor   bright

As an introduction to the song, sing this melody on "doo" or play it on an instrument.

Play the chords on autoharp, ukelele, banjo, or guitar with strong accents on beats 2 and 4.

Old-fashioned tempo!

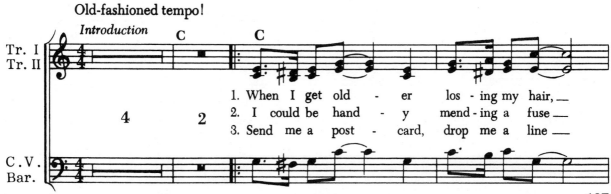

1. When I get old - er los - ing my hair, __
2. I could be hand - y mend - ing a fuse __
3. Send me a post - card, drop me a line __

Copyright © 1967 Northern Songs Limited. All rights reserved. Used by permission.

man-y years from now, ___ will you still be send-ing me a
when your lights have gone, ___ you can knit a sweat-er by the
stat-ing point of view. ___ In-di-cate pre-cise-ly what you

val-en-tine, ___ birth-day greet-ings, bot-tle of wine? ___
fire-side, ___ Sun-day morn-ings go for a ride. ___
mean to say, ___ yours sin-cere-ly wast-ing a-way. ___

If I'd been out ___ till quar-ter to three, ___
Do-ing the gar-den, dig-ging the weeds, ___
Give me your an-swer, fill in a form: ___

would you lock the door? ___
who could ask for more? ___
mine for ev-er-more. ___
Will you still need ___ me,

3rd time to Coda ✛

will you still feed ___ me when I'm six-ty-

188

Sing on 2nd verse only (1st verse tacet) — — — — — — — — — —

C   **Am**

four?   2. Ev - ery sum - mer we can rent a cot - tage in the Isle of Wight,

Sing on 1st verse only (2nd verse tacet) —

1. Oo ____

G — — — — — —   **Am** — —

if it's not too dear. ____   1. Ah ____

(2.) We shall scrimp and

(1.) You'll be old - er

2. We shall scrimp and

E7   **E7**   **Am**   **Dm**

                Ah ____

save. ____   Ah ____

too, ____   and if you say the word, ____

save. ____   Grand - chil - dren on your knee: ____

F   **G7**   **C**   ✛ *Coda*   **C**

(1.) I could stay with you.

(2.) Ve - ra, Chuck, and Dave.

four? (Ho!)   4

I WISH I KNEW HOW IT WOULD FEEL
TO BE FREE

Arranged by Buryl Red

Music by Billy Taylor
Words by Billy Taylor
and Dick Dallas

An important musical device used in this song is the frequent repetition of the same rhythmic patterns. Locate examples. Why do you think the composer used this device?

Accompany the song with these instrumental patterns to provide a foundation and contrast to the dominant rhythm.

Drums or Hand Claps

Tambourines or Finger Snaps

Moderate Gospel tempo

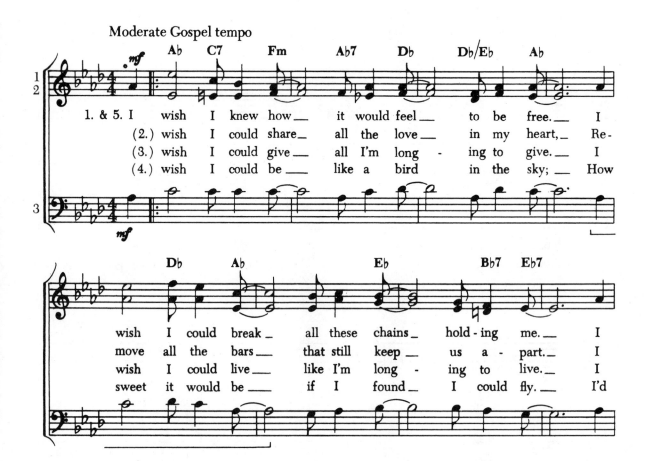

1. & 5. I wish I knew how __ it would feel __ to be free. __ I
(2.) wish I could share __ all the love __ in my heart, __ Re-
(3.) wish I could give __ all I'm long - ing to give. __ I
(4.) wish I could be __ like a bird in the sky; __ How

wish I could break __ all these chains __ hold-ing me. __ I
move all the bars __ that still keep __ us a - part. __ I
wish I could live __ like I'm long - ing to live. __ I
sweet it would be __ if I found __ I could fly. __ I'd

Copyright © 1964 and 1968 by Duane Music, Inc. Reprinted by permission of the publisher.

wish I could say ___ all the things ___ I should say, ___ Say 'em loud, ___
wish you could know ___ what it means ___ to be me; ___ Then you'd see ___
wish I could do ___ all the things ___ I can do; ___ Though I'm 'way ___
soar to the sun ___ and look down ___ at the sea; ___ Then I'd sing, ___

___ say 'em clear, ___ for the whole ___ world to hear. ___ 2. I
___ and a - gree, ___ ev - ery man ___ should be free. ___ 3. I
___ o - ver - due, ___ I'd be start - ing a - new. ___ 4. I
___ 'cause I'd know ___ how it feels ___ to be free. ___ 5. I

5.   *f*   *ritard.*

___ Say 'em loud, ___ say 'em clear, _____ for the

whole wide world to hear. _____

HAVA NAGILA

Arranged by Buryl Red

Jewish Folk Song

"Hava Nagila" is one of the most popular melodies used for dancing the **hora,** a traditional Israeli folk dance. The hora is danced in a circle, arms linked at shoulders. The basic pattern is six beats long and always moves to the left.

Beat 1: Side step to left with left foot.
Beat 2: Cross right foot in back of left foot.
Beat 3: Side step to left with left foot.
Beat 4: Hop on left foot as you kick right foot in front.
Beat 5: Step on right foot.
Beat 6: Hop on right foot as you kick left foot in front.

Practice thinking "left, right, left, hop, right, hop."

Try some of these variations and improvise your own.

- Dance in two circles, one inside the other, going in opposite directions.
- Dance in several small circles in different parts of the room.
- Stand still and clap with the music while one couple or a small group dances the hora in the center.
- All join hands and raise arms overhead as you run to the center; lower hands as you back out.
- All join hands with arms upraised and circle with a light, running step as a soloist weaves in and out around the circle.

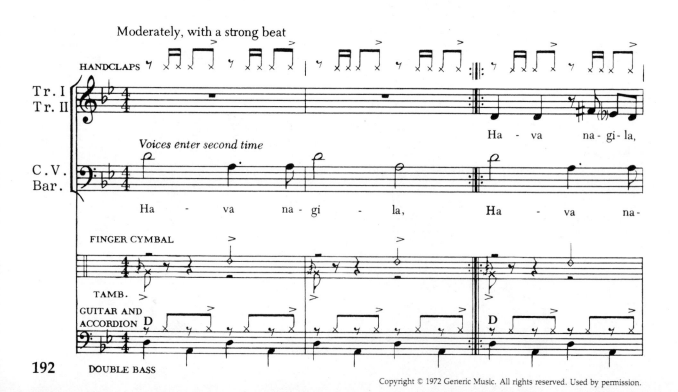

192   DOUBLE BASS

Copyright © 1972 Generic Music. All rights reserved. Used by permission.

ha - va na - gi - la, Ha - va na - gi - la V' - nis m' - cha.

gi - la, Ha - va na - gi - la,

A little faster

Ha - va n' - ra - n' - na, ha - va n' - ra - n' na, Ha - va n' - ra - n' - na

V' - nis m'-cha.   U - ru   u - ru - a - chim

u - ru - a - chim   b'- lev sa - me - ach, U - ru - a - chim   b'- lev sa - me - ach,

U - ru - a - chim b' - lev sa - me - ach, U - ru - a - chim b' - lev sa - me - ach,

U - ru - a - chim u - ru - a - chim b' - lev sa - me - - - ach. _____

Add this part on a wind instrument.

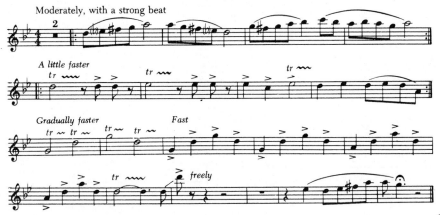

GREEN, GREEN GRASS OF HOME

Arranged by Buryl Red

Words and music by Curly Putman

Copyright © 1965. Reprinted by permission of the publisher, Tree Publishing Co., Inc.

Country music often combines elements of several styles. Which elements do you find in this arrangement?

Gospel
- "amen" cadence at the end of the song
- solo "fills" on piano at end of phrases
- antiphonal effect between soloist and chorus

Nashville sound
- chromatic embellishment of chords in accompaniment

- bass and steel guitars

Add chromatic embellishments on piano or other instruments using the ideas shown above.

197

SULIRAM

Adapted and arranged by Buryl Red

Indonesian Folk Song
English words by
Virginia Stroh Red

Copyright © 1971 by Buryl A. Red. All rights reserved. Used by permission.

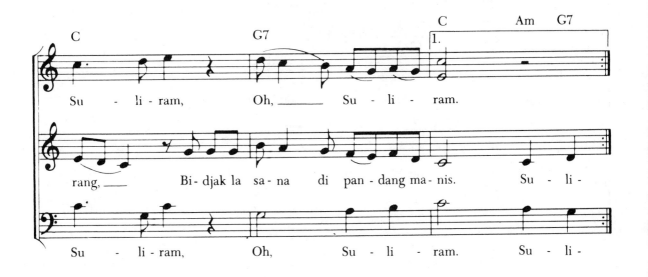

Su - li - ram, Oh, _____ Su - li - ram.

rang, _____ Bi - djak la sa - na di pan - dang ma - nis. Su - li -

Su - li - ram, Oh, Su - li - ram. Su - li -

ram. _____ Slowly and freely Oo _____

nis. _____ Hush now, my ba - by, the long day is

ram. _____ Oo _____

Su - li - ram. Oo _____

past, Su - li - ram. Let sleep en - fold you and dreams come at

Su - li - ram. Oo _____

199

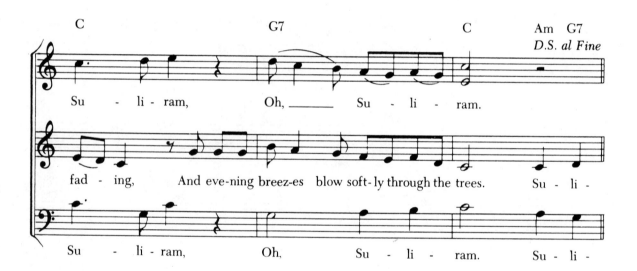

Although this is an Indonesian melody, it shows the influence of western European musical styles. Research the history of Indonesia to discover how this mixture of styles may have occurred.

Which of these characteristics do you feel most reflects the influence of western Europe? Indonesia?

major tonality   **irregular phrase length**
frequent repetition   **flexible rhythmic structure**

Review the discussion of the gamelan, the Indonesian orchestra, on page 87. Develop a gamelan-type accompaniment to "Suliram" by playing any or all of the parts suggested on page 203.

GOOD MORNING STARSHINE

Arranged by Fred Bock

Music by Galt MacDermot
Words by James Rado and Gerome Ragni

Copyright © 1966, 1967, 1968 James Rado, Gerome Ragni, Galt MacDermot, Nat Shapiro and United Artists Music Co., Inc.
All rights administered by United Artists Music Co., Inc., New York, New York 10019. Used by permission.

FIVE HUNDRED MILES

Arranged by Buryl Red

Words and Music by Hedy West

Compare this arrangement of "Five Hundred Miles" to the one that you developed on page 61. What are the similarities? differences? Study the score before you learn this arrangement.

Locate the passages where the melody and harmonizing parts:

- have the same words and rhythm;
- have contrasting words and rhythm.

"Word painting" is a musical device sometimes used by composers to add interest to their compositions. The musical sounds specifically suggest the word meaning. Locate examples of word painting in this arrangement.

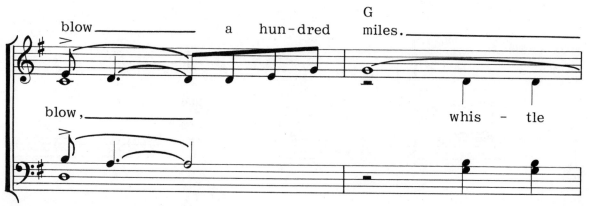

Lord, I'm five hundred
three,___ Lord, I'm four, five hundred

miles___ a - way from home.___
miles,___ 'way from

Refrain

home.___ A-way from home, a-way from home, a-way from

home, a-way from home,
five hundred

EVERYTHING IS BEAUTIFUL

Arranged by Fred Bock

Words and Music by Ray Stevens

Copyright © 1970 by Ahab Music Company, Inc. Words and music by Ray Stevens. Used by permission.

see, ___ We must not close our minds, ___ we must let our thoughts be

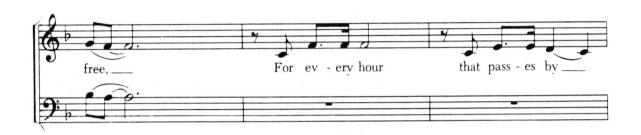

free, ___ For ev - ery hour that pass - es by ___

you know the world gets a lit - tle bit old - er; It's time to re - al - ize

D.S. al Coda

(no breath)

that beau-ty lies in the eyes ___ of the be - hold - er. And ev-ery-thing is

(no breath)

⊕ *Coda*

ff
(one soprano)

Un - der God's heav - en, the world's gon-na find ___ a way, find a way.

ff

GOD'S GOIN' TO SET THIS WORLD ON FIRE

Arranged by William Grant Still

Spiritual

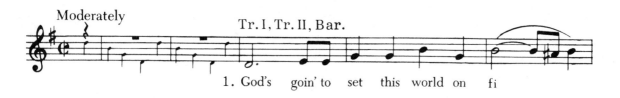

Moderately
Tr. I, Tr. II, Bar.

1. God's goin' to set this world on fi

yah, God's goin' to set this world on fi - yah One of these

days, Hal - le - lu - jah! God's goin' to set this world on fi -

yah, God's goin' to set this world on fi - yah one of these days.

Descant Tr. I, C.V.

2. I'm goin' to climb up Ja - cob's lad - der, I'm goin' to

Melody Tr. II, Bar.

climb up Ja - cob's lad - der on - a that day, Hal - le - lu - jah! I'm goin' to

climb up Ja - cob's lad - der, I'm goin' to climb up Ja - cob's

Tr. I, Tr. II

lad - der on - a that day.

C.V., Bar.

3. God don't

want no cow - ard sol - diers, God don't want no cow - ard

gradually slower

sol - diers none of these days, Hal - le - lu - jah! God don't want no cow - ard

slower

sol - diers, God don't want no cow- ard sol-diers none of these days. ____

THE TREE OF PEACE

Adapted by Fred Bock
Words from "O Brother Man" by John Greenleaf Whittier

Music by Fred Bock

The lyrics of this song were adapted from a poem written in 1848 by the famous American poet, John Greenleaf Whittier. Read the words aloud as a poem. Observe the expressive indications provided within the score.

How do the dynamics, articulation, and entirely homophonic setting help to express the mood of the words?

Copyright © 1970 by Gentry Publications, Tarzana, California. International copyright secured.
All rights reserved. Used by permission.

hymn, each kind - ly deed a prayer. ____

Girls: second time only.

Then shall all the shack - les fall off ____ and the storm - y clang - or of

f (Boys both times)

war's wild mu - sic o'er the earth shall cease! earth shall cease! ____

a little slower

Love shall put out the burn - ing fire of an - ger,

And in its ash - es plant the tree of peace, And in its

ash - es plant the tree, plant the tree of peace! ____

IF WE DON'T MAKE IT WORK, WHO WILL?

Lyrics by Grace Hawthorne

Music by Buryl Red

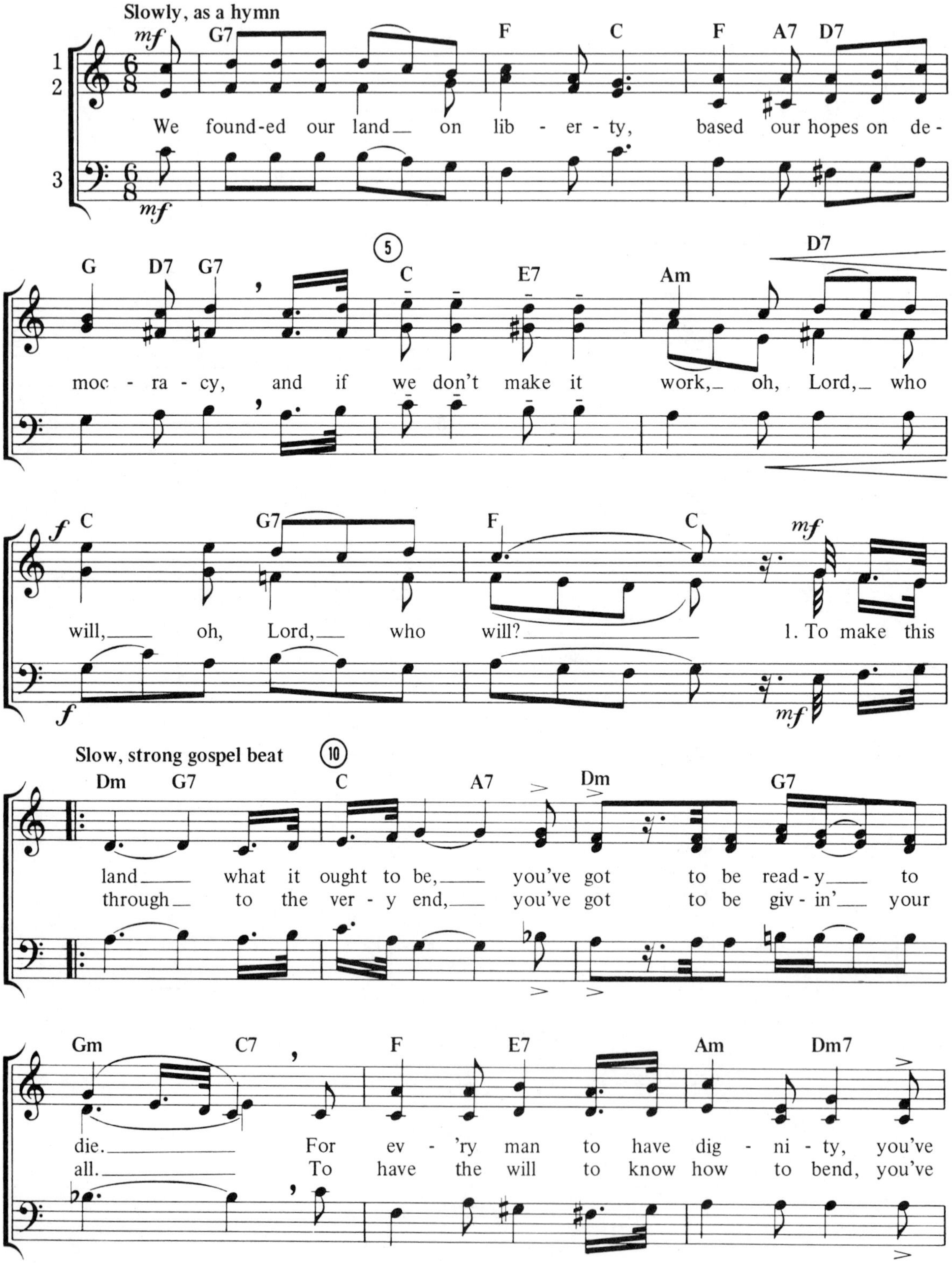

Slowly, as a hymn
mf
G7 F C F A7 D7
We found-ed our land on lib - er - ty, based our hopes on de -
G D7 G7 C E7 Am D7
moc - ra - cy, and if we don't make it work, oh, Lord, who
f C G7 F C mf
will, oh, Lord, who will? 1. To make this
Slow, strong gospel beat
Dm G7 C A7 Dm G7
land what it ought to be, you've got to be read - y to
through to the ver - y end, you've got to be giv - in' your
Gm C7 F E7 Am Dm7
die. For ev - 'ry man to have dig - ni - ty, you've
all. To have the will to know how to bend, you've

Copyright © 1974, Trigon Music, Inc. All rights reserved. Used by permission.

BELL GLORIA

Music by Buryl Red

Perform this composition in a random manner to suggest the sound of carillon bells ringing out. Each part should establish its *own* underlying beat and need not attempt to perform in exact rhythmic relationship with the other parts. Begin with Bell Pattern A followed by Bell Pattern B, then Hand Bells. Vocal Parts then enter one by one, in any order. Repeat indefinitely!

Ring these notes at random in any octave.

Improvise other parts of your own on these notes of the pentatonic scale.

218

Copyright © 1970 by Generic Music. All rights reserved. Used by permission.

Alphabetical Index